PHILOSOPHERS

*Exploring Ideas through
the Study of Six Great Lives*

from the Creative Lives Series

By Margaret M. Madigan
Edited by Sally J. Patton

Zephyr Press
Tucson, Arizona

PHILOSOPHERS
Exploring Ideas through the Study of Six Great Lives

Grades 5–12

© copyright 1977, Patton Pending
© copyright 1992, Revised Edition, Zephyr Press

ISBN: 0-913705-34-9

Illustrator: Laurie Hobson
Educational Consultant: Shirley Schiever, Ph.D.

Zephyr Press
P.O. Box 13448
Tucson, Arizona 85732-3448

The purchase of this book entitles the individual teacher to reproduce student activities for use in the classroom. All rights reserved. The reproduction of any part for an entire school or school system or for commercial use is strictly prohibited. No form of this work may be reproduced or transmitted or recorded without written permission from the publisher.

FOREWORD

By natural inclination students turn toward models, not for definition but for direction; if no models are made available, students often unwittingly choose the first image encountered. The world faces impending and wary crossroads. For these reasons we asked: How does a teacher present great minds and souls to a student but at the same time elicit the student's commitment to discover his or her own unique voice? How does a teacher hold up a mirror of human potential but avoid encouraging an intellect which merely emulates or mimics? How does the courage to discover and live, to *realize* our own destiny, occur?

These were some of the concerns that influenced this Source Guide. Knowing childhood and adolescence to be critical stages in our students' growth, that is, times of challenge and identity-seeking, we included herein some of the healthiest, most integrated and self-actualized* people. Prerequisites for selection depended on their rich personal and social lives, the availability of materials, and their ability to speak to us across culture, space, and time. The individuals chosen contributed their own design, purpose, message, and incredible energy. The Guide was, therefore, more jointly written than at first glance suspected, for the spirit of these people lives on and manifests itself within these pages.

TO THE TEACHER

Philosophers is a learning center within a book. The first part of the book gives you, the teacher, in-depth background information on the subject itself as well as on each of the philosophers to be studied. A generous bibliography gives easy access to rich resources for your classroom. We hope you'll add to this list resources of your own: posters, music, filmstrips, and artifacts that will excite your students about philosophy and philosophers. Designate a special section of the classroom with chairs, tables, the resources, and bulletin boards and give ample time for browsing.

Several student assignments are included for each of the philosophers. Reproduce the assignments, then cut each one out separately. Glue each assignment onto a piece of colored tagboard that has been cut in a shape of your choice. Create a shape to fit the subject or, better yet, have your students create the pattern shape.

*Abraham Maslow, The Farther Reaches of Human Nature (Esalen Books, Viking Press, New York, 1962)

You decide how many of the assignments each student should complete, then let the students select their own based on their interest and enthusiasm. A real value for the students is to have the opportunity to read and consider all the assignments and then choose their own. They will learn as they read and perhaps find a new interest or direction to pursue.

Effective Use of Philosophers

This book contains a wealth of information that the teacher and the students can draw on, as well as a variety of tasks to facilitate student learning. As with any method or the use of any tool, the end result or product depends on correct and careful use. These pages are designed to help teachers enhance and facilitate students' learning. The following are offered to this end:

1. Review the tasks provided to check for skills that need to be taught before beginning the unit. For example, many students do not know how to evaluate according to criteria. Therefore, the teacher's task is to provide information and practice in developing criteria and using them to evaluate ideas. Rank ordering and providing reasons to support the order may be new to students; comparing and contrasting, which requires finding similarities *and* differences, may also need to be taught.

2. The purpose of the tasks is to require students to process information, or to use the higher levels of thinking. A knowledge base is critical to higher level thinking, and the teacher must establish that students have sufficient information on the topic before they choose tasks.

3. The tasks in this book are based on Bloom's Taxonomy of Cognitive Objectives and Krathwohl's Taxonomy of Affective Objectives, which are hierarchical models. A hierarchical model of thinking requires a sequential movement through the steps, as each level builds on the preceding one. While disagreement exists regarding whether evaluation requires a higher level of thinking than synthesis, students must recall, understand and be able to apply and analyze information and concepts before they can engage in synthesis or evaluative thinking. Requiring students to complete a task at each level is not necessary if the teacher employs some means to ensure the existence of the necessary depth of understanding.

4. Evaluation of student learning, progress, and products is important. Such evaluation should provide the student, teacher, administrator, and parent with information about the learning that is occuring. One way to evaluate is for the teacher to develop general criteria for all students, based on district and program goals, and allow each student to develop (usually in conjunction with teacher and perhaps parent input) specific criteria that he or she wants to have included in the evaluation. When possible, the evaluation should include persons in addition to the teacher and the student. Other school personnel or community members may be appropriate for the evaluation of some products.

5. A synthesis of each topic covered in this book is provided, and may be used as background information for the teacher and/or students. Gathering an abundance of other resources is critical to the successful use of this book. Students need the experience of gathering information from a variety of sources, especially if the sources differ in viewpoint or even "facts" presented.

6. In each section, the pages titled with the philosopher's name and Transpersonal Domain could be used in a learning center, or copied for each student for extra work in class or to take home. Read the section on Meditation and Transpersonal Domain at the end of the book for background information.

7. Many of the tasks and suggested products herein are oriented toward verbal expression. Encourage students to find other ways to illustrate their ideas or what they've learned; ways that reflect their personal learning styles or modes of expression. Additionally, encourage them to use a variety of media to express themselves and to be (or become) risk-takers in occasionally choosing the unfamiliar.

Good Luck—may you and your students learn and grow from the use of these materials!

TABLE OF CONTENTS

GENESIS 7
THE PHILOSOPHY OF THIS GUIDE 9
GOALS OF THE UNIT 10
HOW DO WE KNOW WHAT WE KNOW? 11

BUDDHA 14
    Vocabulary 20
    Transpersonal Domain 21
    Activities 22
    Bibliography 25
    Resources for Teachers 26

SOCRATES, PLATO, ARISTOTLE 28
    Vocabulary 39
    Transpersonal Domain 40
    Activities 41
    Bibliography 43
    Resources for Teachers 44

HENRY DAVID THOREAU 46
    Vocabulary 53
    Transpersonal Domain 54
    Activities 55
    Bibliography 57
    Resources for Teachers 58

MOHANDAS K. GANDHI 61
    Vocabulary 70
    Transpersonal Domain 71
    Activities 72
    Bibliography 74
    Resources for Teachers 75

RACHEL CARSON 78
    Vocabulary 84
    Transpersonal Domain 85
    Activities 86
    Bibliography 88
    Resources for Teachers 88

MARTIN LUTHER KING, JR. 90
    Vocabulary 100
    Transpersonal Domain 101
    Activities 102
    Bibliography 104
    Resources for Teachers ... 105

GENERAL RESOURCES 107
TAXONOMY OF COGNITIVE OBJECTIVES 111
TAXONOMY OF AFFECTIVE OBJECTIVES 111
MEDITATION AND THE TRANSPERSONAL DOMAIN 112
COGNITIVE, AFFECTIVE, AND TRANSPERSONAL DOMAINS 117

GENESIS

What is philosophy? If that were really the first question, the answer would be easy. An intellectual research could be initiated to plagiarize someone else's answer as if philosophy itself were an entity and separate from each of us. A pandora's box could be labeled "Philosophy" and locked away in an ancient house of learning, strangling pursuit that is reserved for the heady and few but is not relevant to the public domain.

But it *isn't* the first question. Philosophy is as much a part of each of us as are breathing, eating, seeing. It is the metaphorical journey in all the children's books, written, ironically, for adults. It is a journey unavoidable and challenging. It is a journey that we embark upon with the young people we encounter every school day. Between the sun's rise and set each day are held a teaching and a call to choice with the responsibility to realize choice within action, to realize the self within life.

The culmination each of us reaches at the end of this search is no less meaningful or critical than it was for Buddha or Gandhi or Rachel Carson. They were merely doing what we all are doing, not seeking a philosophy but *being*. Is philosophy just being, then? Is this the first question? How to be? Is this being a patternless, random journey through choice after choice? Are we merely an audience or are we involved in how we emerge? It must be remembered here that philosophy, the love or pursuit of knowledge, is only a word. A word symbolizes a process. A process is rooted in reality, in the now. It is actually the moment-to-moment simultaneous creation and discovery of who we indeed, *in deed*, are. In realty *being* is an active verb (in the highest sense).

Questions are asked and answers found during this process. Some are individual and personal. Some are universal and shared. Who am I? From where does my identity flourish: from myself, from my friends, from my parents, from my profession, from God? What is this God's nature? What is reality? Is reality the same for us all? Does an animal have a soul? What is the soul? What responsibility do I have toward myself, toward society, toward man, toward earth? Can I know all these things in a logical, permanent way? Will I discover my answers as I live? Who I am?

These are the first questions. In asking all this we demonstrate our first step into human consciousness. This is a consciousness that we are indeed alive and aware. We can choose to some extent reality. This is the first motion towards the self-knowledge, the individual self of the universal self, which Socrates bade us to know, rather be. Socrates merely stated the

Genesis

challenge to know the self, but the question is generic to each of us. It is the same self that Buddha, Socrates, Gandhi, Thoreau, Martin Luther King, Jr., and Rachel Carson pursued. They represented the epitome not only of what is the true individual but also of the actor committed to his or her part in the universal pathos. This pathos is the human's pursuit of truth, not in an abstract sense one can always explain, but the truth in the moment or the truth in our conscience. *This* is philosophy and we are the philosophers.

This Source Guide has been written to make this real to us. The six individuals selected are mirrors of our own potential real selves—not so much the specifics of their lives, but the commitment and integrity they exemplify. They were always looking at the world and themselves as part of that world, meditating, questioning, receiving, transforming themselves. As they discovered, they appreciated, they valued, they believed.

These are all actions. By their beliefs transmitted into action they lived their limited answers in their everyday lives. In their loving, in their writing, in their teaching, they evolved towards their ultimate concerns, concerns whose answers shook the universe and changed man and woman for all time. Neither fame nor the attacks against their fortunes or reputations or persons could dissuade them from their own being and perception of the world as they saw it. Though the light they bore evidenced a facet of their own times and early influences, one is overwhelmed that these people represent more than a reflection of or reaction to the status quo. They responded to the outside world, but also moved from an inner purpose and realization. From Buddha to Carson, they were all eventual dissenters from their culture involved in one form or another of civil disobedience. Yet they were visionaries, apt in perceiving what existed and knowing deeply the unacceptable. They lived and pursued the reality or 'dream' that they believed 'in truth' could exist here and now for all.

These men and women took great risks, regardless of what had existed or was currently fashionable. Above all, they held a reverence for all life, attending to it in the moment. Philosophy, then, the love or pursuit of knowledge, knowledge being truth, is in the moment. Philosophy is ever present yet evolving, always complete yet growing. Philosophy is, at death, yet another realization accumulated in retrospect of what *in deed* we have become.

THE PHILOSOPHY OF THIS GUIDE

In the realist sense, then, all education is centered around the bid to know thyself. From this premise, it follows that the actual investigation of philosophy should be more than a study of the questions and answers of others. Though much is to be gained in guidance by their courage and individuality, the challenge lies in eliciting from students their own involvement as individuals in reality.

This Guide aims toward this goal and offers the biographical sketches and extended reading to support but never supplant the experiences. Both the Cognitive and Affective Domains integrate here. They create a third domain: the Transpersonal Domain. If we can view the Affective Domain as the individual and the Cognitive Domain as its tool, we have a better opportunity to allow this Guide to expose rather than to lead. If it succeeds, the first questions which characterize philosophy will be asked in terms of one's own life.

As far as our screening devices can demonstrate, the students who best qualify for involvement possess the ability to analyze and value not only the abstract truths but also the personal realities of the people in this Guide. They also have the potential for a higher degree of creative individuality and leadership. The definition of leadership (able to lead one's self) seems appropriate here. Then social and political leadership might evolve. These being our present beliefs, the goals of this Guide are related to the potentialities we have defined for the gifted/talented student. Regardless of the arena in which this potential is displayed—music, art, politics, religion—a knowledge of themselves, the world, and others of the past and present can assist such students in developing the courage to become what they are.

A word here about your own involvement as an individual. How does a teacher share without leading? Partly by his or her own enthusiasm and joy, partly by sharing insights which erupt spontaneously, as an individual, not necessarily as a teacher but as a part of your own process. Also, if you never feel a little afraid or uncertain guiding the experiences in the unit, being insecure, you're failing somewhere. Don't expect to feel completely 'on top' of it all the time.

All of the people presented in this Guide left collections of prosaic and voluminous writing. Some they wrote themselves, others were transcribed by their disciples. It is helpful to initiate journal-keeping at the onset of this Guide for yourself as well as for your students. Many of the students' responses require writing. Many of the activities may inspire them to write about

Goals of the Unit

insights and feelings. If the introduction is accepted seriously, that we all, teacher and student alike, are part of this journey, can we in good conscience ask our students to do what we ourselves are not willing to do? The journal can let the conscience have its dialogues where it can be itself, a private place to be shared.

The emphasis on these philosophers as writers of journals and books is crucial since this is a valuable source for appreciating their realities and risks. For them as for us, perhaps it is like practicing the piano was to Mozart, or sketching was to Van Gogh, or scratching a schematic was to Leonardo. What is expressed is remembered. It can be shared, developed, and transformed into action. What becomes action becomes real. What becomes real has the power to transform ourselves and the selves of others.

GOALS OF THE UNIT

GENERAL GOALS OF THE UNIT

The general purposes of this Source Guide are:
- To develop an individual's awareness that Socrates' bid 'Know Thyself' applies to all of us.
- To develop an appreciation of certain philosophers' acceptance of this bid whether or not they knew of Socrates.
- To develop an understanding of the self or philosophy which developed as a result of the acceptance of this bid.
- To develop the ability to recognize the philosophy or being in one's self and in others.
- To distinguish the person from the truths that he/she actualized.

SPECIFIC GOALS OF THE UNIT

The specific purposes of this Source Guide are that gifted/talented pupils will:
- Understand and express their own valuing, believing, and being.
- Evidence more mature intellectual and emotional responses to the being and philosophy of themselves and others.
- View and respect the 'great people' of the past as 'others' with the courage to be and share what was unique to them and what was universal.
- Appreciate and distinguish the being or philosophy of the people in this Source Guide.
- Develop a love and understanding of the importance of the process or journey that we are all involved in as individuals and, especially, as Homo sapiens.

HOW DO WE KNOW WHAT WE KNOW?

There is an ancient Indian fable entitled "The Blind Men and the Elephant"* which, ironically, can be viewed from many perspectives. Three which seem relevant to this Source Guide concern (1) perceptions of reality within the individual; (2) perceptions of reality within a group, a society, the species; and (3) a convincing rationale encouraging receptivity, scrutiny, and transcendance of our own individual opinions as well as those held by other people, religions, and cultures. The prime message suggests, then, that only by putting the pieces together will we approach the true essence of what we are looking at, in our case the self or truth or reality.

In this fable reality is symbolized by an elephant. Six blind men set out to locate and comprehend this thing called 'elephant' of which all have heard but none has seen. They are to be commended for their direct approach through personal experience, but their method proves insufficient. Once they had found the elephant, each one, disregarding his handicap of blindness, supposed that by touching and holding on to one part of the elephant he had indeed apprehended the true essence of elephant. Each clung to his opinion, never listening to the other, only arguing louder and louder. According to the part each had held, one likened the elephant to a wall, another to a snake, another to a spear. Yet another compared it to a tree, the next a fan, and, finally, a rope. The argument continued under the sweltering sun. No one would agree. After much shouting a Rajah, or wise man, called to them. In a calm voice he told them that the elephant was an enormous animal and that each one of them had only touched on one part. If they truly sought to discern the total, they would have to sit and listen to each other, sharing their ideas until they had pieced together the whole, the truth of the elephant.

Though the Rajah himself had the faculty to see and know the elephant, whereas the blind men did not, he pointed the way, explained the process, and allowed them the joy of discovery. Rather than tell them another opinion, though informed, he gave them the greatest gift process.

This story in this Guide seems obvious and will be consistently relevant throughout. Discussion of it can be used as a springboard into the units and a persistent thread to refer to later in terms of each of the lives presented. An initial discussion concerning the uniqueness of perception, perceptions within one individual, a group, a society, our species, can develop an openness to the students' own disparate feelings, to others in the class and their own lives, as

* Lillian Quigley, "The Blind Men and the Elephant" (Charles Scribner's Son's, New York, 1959)

How Do We Know What We Know?

well as to the masters towards which this Guide turns. Conditioning can also be discussed as a kind of blindness, including personal fears and cultural influence. First impressions of the focus we take when we look at something or another person can be searched for their roots in this conditioning. Often our unconscious choices can act as a lens distorting our perceptions of what is real. This distortion can range from grossly distorted, to partially distorted, to fairly holistic or just short of reality. Discussion, games, experiences, visualizations, meditation—all these can help unearth our distortions and demonstrate the 'reality' of the story.

Opening as an individual, or as a people, to looking at one thing long enough to see the many facets, as well as sharing perceptions with others, can be introduced as integral, if not sine qua non, to knowing the individual self, the self of others, perhaps even the human self. The process of sharing is a dialectic, the conversation between two or more points which Socrates discovered. It allows us the chance to evolve and discover who we are, what our place in the universe is, integrating us with that one song.

This opening does not mean we must necessarily give up our values or opinions, but merely suspend solidifying them. Nor does it mean our first perception didn't intuit the essence of what we were scrutinizing. If we did apprehend the truth of it, looking at all sides can only make it richer and easier to understand when someone else gets stuck in a misconception or opinion. Later we can consciously choose and pursue our values, yet remain open. As will be seen, Socrates and Gandhi were masters at this. But all the great philosophers knew that a fully enlightened or holistic value will not disintegrate when faced even with extreme resistance. The difference was that their *knowing* meant *living*. They knew and lived believing that the simple truth would provide the courage to persist and the overall justice if they seemed to fail. Socrates made this choice; Gandhi based his whole life and the life of a nation on it.

This Guide offers some different sides to this thing 'life,' often likened to a maze we all attempt to comprehend as we maneuver our way. None of us knows all the answers, some of us can barely engender even a few questions, many no longer even wonder. Perhaps by listening to and sharing with the spirits of those who speak across culture and space and time, as well as the evolving selves we meet every day, we can touch our own conscience, a being free of conditioning and fear, indeed, a *being* free.

Gautama Buddha

a man is not born to mastery.
a master is never proud.
he does not talk down to others.
owning nothing, he misses nothing.
he is not afraid.
he does not tremble.
nothing binds him.
he is infinitely free.
so cut through
the strap and the thong and the rope.
loosen the fastenings.
unbolt the doors of sleep
and awake.

from: <u>sayings of the buddha</u>

Gautama Buddha

**Gautama Buddha
(560-440 B. C.)**

To many people, Buddhists, religious scholars, even Buddha himself, the Buddha is more a reality than a person, more a goal of truth than the individual attainment, more universal than personal. Though it is believed by the Buddhists that there have been and will be many Buddhas, there is one especially real individual who journeyed the personal life span to realize this eternal spiritual reality. His name was Siddhartha Gautama. Born into 2,500 years of traditional **Brahminism** near what is now Nepal in the year 560 B.C., he was to become like Jesus Christ, a leader of men in a new way.

This way or path, however, developed much later in life. Similiar to Christ, **Siddhartha**, whose name means 'wish fulfillment,' was destined for an extraordinary reality. By the method of fortune telling it was prophesied at birth that Siddhartha would either become a **Buddha**—an **enlightened** one—or a great emperor. This news greatly distressed Siddhartha's family, especially his father, for their family belonged to the **caste** of rulers. To lose one's child to the caste of priests was paralleled to a loss through death. But the Brahmin priest Kondanna 'read' the boy's body. Seeing the golden hue and the perfectly formed limbs, the blue flax of his eyes, Kondanna fell down weeping that he might not live long enough to see the child reach his enlightenment. He told the king, "A time will come when he will witness four special signs and as a result he will renounce the world and go out to seek enlightenment. Eventually he will achieve that enlightenment and become a Buddha." At this Kondanna and four disciples went away to await the day of Siddhartha's enlightenment.

This fear of losing his son caused the king to overprotect and shield Siddhartha from the realities of the world. It was a perfect existence—no hint of death, sickness, hunger, aging. It was an environment which totally denied the realities of the human predicament. An ancient scripture has the coddled child proclaiming, "I had three palaces: one for the cold season, one for the hot, and one for the season of the rains. Through the rainy season, entertained by female minstrels, I did not come down from the palace." An aristocrat of the warrior and ruler class, Siddhartha spent his boyhood, adolescence, and young manhood in this way. He wanted for nothing. He excelled at all he pursued. No troubles invaded his house. His luxury and domestic tranquility were assured. His marriage to the beautiful and delicate Yosadhara brought yet another glorious yield, a son.

Despite this fairy-tale existence, Siddhartha was even as a child quite unique. Good manners and a kindly nature endeared him to servant and ruler alike. Even in this sheltered existence his compassion grew, extending to all living things. He discovered **meditation** naturally and quite early, practiced the breathing and discipline as would a master. He is remembered, much

Gautama Buddha

to his father's heartache, to have said, "... this is my last existence." At this his father became fanatical; even drooping or faded flowers were removed from gardens lest the prince guess the actual process of decay and death inherent to life. Nowhere in that manicured, lush, and tranquil encampment was death, allowed to show its true nature.

Siddhartha was like a tiny jewel growing in this affluence and illusion. With great satisfaction the king watched as his son developed into a strong and capable man, worthy of being an emperor's son. Besides his outstanding intellectual powers and striking beauty, Siddhartha out-distanced all his peers in the martial arts, with archery his favorite. In body and mind he was agile and keen. But something went amiss. Though he possessed all the abilities, wealth, and opportunities most men crave, Siddhartha became thoughtful and preoccupied... bored.

In his middle twenties this boredom became intense curiosity about the outside world. Something seemed to be lacking in his life. From appearances, even he had to admit, he seemed to possess what all men of all generations hunger for. Against his father's wishes and warnings, he escaped by chariot and went out into the world to seek answers. What he found was to horrify and change him profoundly. A new life was to begin.

During this first venture Siddhartha encountered a very old man. He was appalled, not recognizing the decrepit body as a man at first. On later journeys he met a sick man and a dead man. Finally he met a ragged **ascetic**, one who forsakes the physical world for spiritual truth. Siddhartha saw nothing but suffering all around him. Now, even his comfortable existence provided little satisfaction or sanctuary. He knew he could not escape the fate of life and death. Returning to the palace shaken and troubled each time, he pondered all the misery he had encountered. He marveled at the happiness of the ascetic and decided then to leave his illusory existence. True to the prophecy and to the path of **renunciation** common to Brahmins, he left his luxury and entered the world of suffering as a monk, wearing the monastic yellow robe and shaven head and begging for his food. His friends could hardly recognize him when he assumed other guises in his attempt to discover the secrets of life.

This decision to leave was set against the backdrop of much political, religious, and social unrest. It was a time of ferment and experimentation. The traditional rituals and explanations no longer answered or satisfied people. It did not seem right that wisdom should be accessible only through knowledge and preserved just for diligent scholars. Siddhartha challenged this also. Thus his six-year search began.

In his attempt to solve the riddle of life, for neither luxury nor suffering seemed to contain it, Siddhartha spent his days experiencing all extremes of starvation, cold, loneliness, fever, wealth, and indulgence. Finally in utter desperation he sat beneath the banyan tree and vowed not to get up until he had attained the secret of enlightenment. "Let my skin wither, my hands grow numb, my bones dissolve," he said. "Until I have attained understanding I will not rise from here." And he did not. He sat for 49 days entering deeper and deeper into meditation. During this meditation every evil force or **mara** would tempt him, offering him everything: riches, women, power, immortality. They attacked him with passions few men ever experience, hurtling rocks and bits of twisted trees at him. But Siddhartha endured. He wondered amidst all this how things came into being and departed from being. Even when no answer came he sat steadfast, pointing his right hand towards the earth, calling it to witness his ordeal.

And the earth stood by him. Finally after 49 days Siddhartha Gautama stood up from under the banyan tree and looked out upon the world as if for the first time, holding within his heart the secret of enlightenment, the deliverance he had cried out for. "Now the cycle of rebirth is ended for me," he said afterward. "For me this world no longer matters." Thus Siddhartha became Gautama Buddha, the Enlightened One, and traveled throughout the land teaching not the secret, for that must be attained with proper **protocol**, but the 'way,' the **dhamma**, by using parable and living example.

Gautama Buddha became a teacher of great influence. Even today his message has spread to the West. He taught that all that befalls us, the good and the bad, is within our own power to control. Suffering results from desire, and the only remedy is a pure heart. To purify the heart one needs only to pursue the way of truth. Buddha called this the **dhammapada**. Dhamma is law, discipline, justice, virtue, truth, that which binds the world together. Pada means way, path, step, foot. The Dhammapada is the path of virtue or the way of truth through discipline.

There are a few basic ideas that underlie the path which Buddha demonstrated by his life. Some were basic to Brahminism or Buddhism in general. Some were new insights which Gautama Buddha realized and taught in his sermons during the remaining 45 years of his life.

An idea common to Brahminism is that all living creatures follow the cycle of birth, death, and rebirth and that most men must be born into the world over and over until they have achieved enlightenment. This is called **reincarnation**. Another is the concept of **karma**, the cause and effect laws which operate around good and evil and their resulting rewards or punishments that result from our choices. It is influential in later reincarnations.

Gautama Buddha

That ultimately the world is a great container of ignorance and sorrow is yet another idea which leads to the advice that the human being should pursue enlightenment and release from the world's fetters. Mentioned earlier, renunciation is also basic to Buddhism. It is the idea that the wise person seeks to subdue the desires and passions of the flesh by freely choosing restriction so that spiritual progress becomes an open channel.

Gautama Buddha was in agreement with these tenets, but his path advised the **middle way**, the avoidance of extremes, the road between self-indulgence and asceticism in a life of calm detachment. The Buddha believed that all men had equal chance in achieving enlightenment, a disagreement with the Brahmin caste system. This caste system separated people into exclusive groups with special privileges given to some and not to others. Beyond these guidelines, Buddha depicted a path based on common sense and compassion, avoidance of ill will, malicious talk, lust, and the harming of any living creature. But most notable of all was the dhammapada that Buddha outlined in the **Four Noble Truths** and the **Noble Eightfold Path**. If these were followed, one would reach Buddhahood and thus **nirvana**.

The Four Noble Truths: 1. Suffering is universal. 2. The cause of suffering is craving or selfish desire. 3. The cure for suffering is the elimination of craving. 4. The way to eliminate craving is to follow the middle way, whose techniques are demonstrated in the Noble Eightfold Path.

The Noble Eightfold Path:
1. Right Knowledge or Understanding—seeing life as it is.
2. Right Intention or Right Thought—a pure or purged mind.
3. Right Speech—one's words reflect one's thoughts.
4. Right Conduct or Action—disciplines which are important to attain enlightenment.
5. Right Means of Livelihood or Occupation—earning one's living in a way consistent with the Path.
6. Right Effort—cultivation of noble qualities.
7. Right Mindfulness—developing intellectual awareness only in service of spiritual progress.
8. Right Concentration or Meditation—the practice of the discipline of meditation.

Between the moment of Buddha's enlightenment at age 35 and his death at 80, the Buddha traveled about converting or transforming people, even his own father, wife, son, and mother. Fulfilling the role of **bodhisattva**, a person who delays his or her entrance into the final realm of nirvana in order to teach and lead others to their salvation, Buddha walked the land speaking freely to those who had ears to hear. During this stage he instructed with sayings intended to guide us. In a collection of sayings which his disciples later wrote down and called *The Dhammapada*, Buddha attempted to help us in the daily pursuit through the maze.

Beginning with a type of invitation to journey, using choice and discipline as the process by which we progress, the Buddha carries us through wakefulness, the mind, the flowers, the fool, the wise man, the master, the thousands. He explores also mischief, violence, old age, the self, and the world. In detail he discusses the man who is awake; he speaks of joy, pleasure, anger, impurity, and the just, and reminds us of the way. Once we see the way and come out of the forest, come out of the dark towards the light, he compares us to the elephant hauling itself out of the mud, but reminds us not to fall asleep again for desire is a great intoxicator. This is a point of beginning, not the end. The seeker seeks always the true, the good, the pure, becoming finally his or her own true master. In *The Dhammapada*, then, Buddha begins by pointing out:

> We are what we think.
> All that we are arises with our thoughts.
> With our thoughts we make the world.
> Speak or act with an impure mind
> And trouble will follow you
> As the wheel follows the ox that draws the cart.
>
> We are what we think.
> All that we are arises with our thoughts.
> With our thoughts we make the world.
> Speak or act with a pure mind
> And happiness will follow you
> As your shadow, unshakable.

Near the middle of these teachings, though, he tells us that we are not ultimately only our thoughts, but that there is an essence capable of choosing and evolving while we are on the Eightfold Path. Once this essence has the capacity to control or stop thought, we become aligned with becoming what we are, aligned with what all life is ultimately. Thus Buddha's final saying from *The Dhammapada*:

Gautama Buddha

He has come to the end of the way.
Over the river of his many lives,
His many deaths.

Beyond the sorrow of hell,
Beyond the great joy of heaven
By virtue of his purity.

He has come to the end of his way.
All that he had to do he has done,
And now he is one.

This was the gift, the path that Buddha left to us. Through meditation in the pursuit of inner knowledge he discovered that the secret is not a goal for a select few via esoteric wisdom, but that the deliverance and freedom man seeks are from within. It is the way, Buddha said, the only way the individual can follow to end suffering and attain **nirvana** or emptiness, a perfect harmony with the universe. In Gautama Buddha's last words, after he had eaten some poisoned food, he reminded us to "Seek the impersonal for the eternal man, and having sought him out, look inward—thou art Buddha."

Vocabulary:

Buddha	ascetic	bodhisattva
mara	meditation	Brahminism
karma	enlightened	Four Noble Truths
dhamma	middle way	Noble Eightfold Path
caste	Siddhartha	renunciation
nirvana	dhammapada	protocol
		reincarnation

Buddha: Transpersonal Domain:
Contemplate at separate sittings.

Contemplate the Buddha.

Read and contemplate the Dhammapada.

Contemplate the Four Noble Truths.

Contemplate the Eightfold Path.

Contemplate a picture or statue of the Buddha.

Contemplate young Siddhartha and his journey.

During your daily meditation and your insight about your own self, remember Buddha's life, the way he taught, and his goal of Nirvana. Remember to see life as it is and to follow your own path.

Gautama Buddha

ACTIVITIES:
COGNITIVE DOMAIN
Knowledge—Comprehension—Application—Analysis—Synthesis—Evaluation

BUDDHA
Knowledge—Cognitive Domain
Describe the men the young Siddhartha met when he ventured from his palace and the change this made in his thinking.

BUDDHA
Comprehension—Cognitive Domain
Explain why these encounters were a shock to young Siddhartha. List three questions he might have asked the old man, the sick man and the ascetic.

BUDDHA
Application—Cognitive Domain
Dramatize a conversation about Siddhartha between the old man and the sick man. Dramatize a conversation between Siddhartha and the ascetic.

BUDDHA
Analysis—Cognitive Domain
Compare Siddhartha's life with that of the ascetic. What similiarities and differences were there between their lives?

BUDDHA
Synthesis—Cognitive Domain
Siddhartha looked for the answer to the riddle of life in luxury, suffering, and meditation. In what ways might contemporary people look for the meaning of life?

BUDDHA
Evaluation—Cognitive Domain
How necessary was Siddhartha's decision to leave his family so he could find the meaning of life? Give three reasons that support your response.

BUDDHA
Knowledge —Cognitive Domain
List on a chart all the similarities and differences between Buddha's Path and traditional Brahminism.

BUDDHA
Comprehension—Cognitive Domain
Explain how religious beliefs affect people's lives. Choose a specific person or belief system to illustrate your explanation.

BUDDHA
Application—Cognitive Domain
In what ways would your life change if you were to follow Buddha's path. Why would each change occur or be necessary?

BUDDHA
Analysis—Cognitive Domain
Compare and contrast the beliefs of your own or another religion with those of Buddha's Path.

BUDDHA
Synthesis—Cognitive Domain
Develop a code of living that is appropriate for contemporary society. Project what life would be like in 20 years if everyone lived by your code.

BUDDHA
Evaluation—Cognitive Domain
List 5 standards of Buddha's Path. On a scale of 1 to 5, with 5 meaning you meet the standard, evaluate your life. Explain why you do or do not want to meet each standard you listed.

Gautama Buddha

AFFECTIVE DOMAIN
Receiving—Responding—Valuing—Organizing—Characterizing

BUDDHA
Receiving—Affective Domain
Close your eyes for 15 minutes (then later for 30 minutes) Listen to Za Zen music, an Indian Raga, sounds of the ocean, a rippling stream, your own heartbeat, or breathing.

BUDDHA
Responding—Affective Domain
Notice all your thoughts as they come and go but don't think hard on any one.

BUDDHA
Valuing—Affective Domain
Relate how you felt before, during, and after the meditation.

BUDDHA
Organizing—Affective Domain
List the many feelings you had and decide which was the strongest and which the weakest, which were positive, which negative, which you resisted, which you were attracted to.

BUDDHA
Characterizing—Affective Domain
Create a poem or a collage of all you experienced during this sitting.

BUDDHA
Receiving—Affective Domain
Listen to, without trying to analyze, *Sayings of the Buddha*, haiku, *Tales of the Dervishes*, or *Tales of the Buddha*.

BUDDHA
Responding—Affective Domain
Write down everything that passes before your mind's eye, noticing the stream of thoughts and images.

BUDDHA
Valuing —Affective Domain
Choose the most appealing thought or image and develop or elaborate on it. What made this thought/image more appealing than others? How did your development or elaboration make it more appealing?

BUDDHA
Organizing—Affective Domain
From the list of thoughts and images, organize from least to most valuable. Explain your ranking.

BUDDHA
Characterizing—Affective Domain
Devise a parable or folktale that illustrates your most valuable idea.

BIBLIOGRAPHY

Title: *The Story of Buddha* (grades 3-10)
Author: Jonathan Landaw
Publisher: Auromere, 1979

Title: *Buddhist Parables*
Author: E.W. Burlingame
Publisher: Krishna Press

Title: *Tao of Pooh*
Author: Benjamin Hoff
Publisher: Pengiun Books, 1983

Title: *Siddhartha* (For older students. May want to read first or censor)
Author: Hermann Hesse
Publisher: New Directions, 1951

Title: *Play With Me*
  (Simple story about receptivity to life)
Author: Marie Hall
Publisher: Puffin Books, 1976

Title: *Cherishing Life* Vol. 2 (grades 3 and up)
Author: Buddhist Text Translation Society Staff
Publisher: Buddhist Text, 1983

Title: *Filiality, the Human Source* Vol. I & 2 (grades 3 and up)
Author: Buddhist Text Translation Society Staff
Publisher: Buddhist Text, 1983

Title: *The Buddhist World* (grades 6 and up)
Author: Anne Bancroft
Publisher: Silver, 1985

FILM

Be Ye Lamps Unto Yourselves

MUSIC

Sounds From Environments Records
Za Zen Meditation Records
Indian Ragas

Gautama Buddha

RESOURCES FOR TEACHERS

Title: *Buddhist Ethics: The Path to Nirvana*
Author: H. Saddhatissa
Publisher: Wisdom Basic Books, 1987

Title: *The Great Religions of the World*
Author: Mary L. Pastva
Publisher: St. Mary's, 1986

Title: *Buddhist Religion: A Historical Introduction*
Author: Robinson and Johnson
Publisher: Wadsworth Publishing, 1982

Title: *Buddha Consciousness*
Author: John Roger
Publisher: Baraka Press, 1976

Title: *Buddhist Philosophy of the Middle Way*
Author: Shoson Miyamoto
Publisher: Buddhist Books, 1983

Title: *Buddhist Philosophy of Thought: Essays in Interpretation*
Author: Alexander Piatigorsky
Publisher: B and N Imports, 1984

Title: *Buddhism: A Select Bibliography*
Author: Satyaprakash
Publisher: South Asia Books, 1986

Title: *Buddha and the Gospel of Buddhism*
Author: Ananda Coomaraswamy
Publisher: Citadel Press, Carol Publishing Group, 1988

Title: *The Buddha* (grades 7 and up)
Author: F.W. Rawding
Publisher: Cambridge University Press, 1975

Title: *What the Buddha Taught*
Author: Walpola Rahula
Publisher: Grove, 1987

Title: *Bhagavad-Gita*
Author: Barbara S. Miller
Publisher: Bantam, 1986

The Greeks: Socrates, Plato, Aristotle

Neglected, the sacred verses rust.
For beauty rusts without use
and unrepaired the house falls into ruin,
and the watch, without vigilance, fails.

In this world and the next
there is impurity and impurity:
when a woman lacks dignity,
when a man lacks generosity.

But the greatest impurity is ignorance.
Free yourself from it.
Be pure.

    From: <u>Sayings of the Buddha</u>

The Greeks: *Socrates, Plato, Aristotle*

Socrates (470 B. C. - 400 B. C.)
Plato (427 B. C. - 348 B. C.)
Aristotle (384 B. C. - 322 B. C.)

The Greeks: Socrates, Plato, Aristotle

Socrates, Plato, Aristotle . . . a trinity of thought, rather spirit, representing the matrix from which emerged Western consciousness from the world of unexamined superstition and myth. These three men are bound together overlapping not only in the proximity of their lives but also in a maturation process of thought. Socrates was the questioner, teacher to the man Plato, as well as a fictitious character recreated by Plato to expound Socrates' ideas and those which Plato later developed himself. Enter Aristotle, student of Plato's academy, who refined, extended, and challenged Plato; thus Socrates.

Though it is still debated and difficult to delineate Socrates from Plato, ultimately it matters little who actually thought of what. It is the idea, content, and spirit being exposed which are important to us. Both Socrates and Plato would agree that it does not matter who happened upon the thought first but rather the light itself contained in the words which stand for a reality.

In order to trace the development of this line of thought, though, we must turn to the individual lives of these men, because they help us relate today to the ideas which were set within very real and human exploration.

First on this horizon was Socrates, an Athenian born in the **deme** of Alopece circa 469 B.C. Considered a homely child, born into a common but not poor family, Socrates was raised in a typical and patriotic home. He received a liberal arts education and was an apprentice to his father's craft of sculpture. Though his father was a much admired stone mason and sculptor, Socrates did not have such a **calling**. He did, however, have a calling within himself which he was aware of from childhood. For always he had this voice within, perhaps what we call **conscience**, something integral to him since birth, something not necessarily taught. Socrates was very much interested in questions of right and wrong. He assumed this inner voice was a divine sign and his source of guidance. A curiosity about the human world ensued. In an age of **open inquiry** and great tolerance, Socrates like many others questioned and discussed every issue which arose. But Socrates was more interested in the nature of a man's **soul** and its cultivation than in the cause of rain as were most of the teachers around him. Whom then could Socrates turn to for teaching?

Looking out into the world he saw many around him in great conflict of opinion about the world and human matters. One, Anaxagoras, born in 500 B.C., made some sense to Socrates. His tenet was that the underlying basis of the universe was **nous** or mind, intellect, or order. To understand the universe one had only to understand the mind to discover the natural order. Beyond this assertion, though, Socrates had little affinity for Anaxagoras, who later was brought to trial for **impiety** when Athens' tolerance for questioners began to decline. Anaxagoras was sentenced to death but escaped and went into exile.

The Greeks: Socrates, Plato, Aristotle

Though Anaxagoras had provided a piece to the puzzle, Socrates felt no closer to the truth. He did believe that he was in right pursuit. Whereas his peers projected all their questions out into the heavens or **cosmos**, he looked within himself and the selves of others. Was he not of nature, and was not the nature of man most worthy of man's scrutiny? Was not the mind of man the maze through which this study must thread? Why question the magnitude of the universe when you are ignorant of your own soul? Thus he turned away from the science of the day to the science of his own soul. If there was no one teaching what he needed to learn, then he would be his own teacher, immersing himself in human discussion to bring to light what was true.

This admission that no one could teach him and that basically he did not know anything was perhaps Socrates' most unique quality. At least he knew he did not know. This was an advantage because he was not tyrannized by his own entrapment in unexamined opinions. The possibility of learning was still open. Since an unexamined life seemed to him not worth living, he set out to examine life, his and anyone's who cared to converse.

Socrates did not use this word "converse" lightly. The method of inquiry known as the **Socratic Method** was based on conversation. The search for truth revolved around the **dialectic**, a process which involves a tension between two points, evolving closer and closer to the truth, or the highest good. He believed that only in debate between these two poles could the confusion of our thoughts be seen, the **contradiction** observed and change made possible once the truth had come to light. This process sharpened our wits, he thought, made us think, rather than cling for years and years to opinions formed in childhood or based on faulty assumptions. There was always an unfolding towards **elenchos**, a refutation, an embarrassment or disgrace where one or both suddenly saw how their own emotional ties to their ideas were created, that the need to defend their ideas, rather than the truth itself, was defense enough. At the point of elenchos the person could become angry and stomp away muttering against Socrates. Many did but, feeling the embarrassment, were grateful for the conviction and the new possibility of learning.

Concentrating on human matters, then, Socrates went out into the world each day, engaging anyone who cared in conversations concerning what was godly and ungodly, beautiful and ugly, just and unjust, prudent and mad, courageous and cowardly. Using questions to pursue the truth, Socrates gave no lectures, nor ever said the other was wrong, but patiently moved the conversation by asking something like, "Now let us see if this is so, . . . or if this is correct." Together they would examine until the contradiction, if it existed, could be seen. Many became very excited and embarrassed. Many became frustrated, for often just when they could admit the opposite of what they once were certain, the conversation would turn another corner making even the opposite idea preposterous. Many would never speak to Socrates again. Others returned repeatedly, hungering for the chance to expose their own contradictions. The contradictions were inherent in thinking itself.

One incident in particular seems representative. During a brief respite from the lengthy war between Athens and Sparta, Socrates was visiting some friends. General Laches was present. Laches was amiable and eager to learn, but not very intelligent. Plato relates the course of the conversation:

"Tell me if you can," Socrates asked, "What is courage?"

"Oh quite easy," said Laches. "A man has courage if he does not run away, but stays at his post and fights against the enemy."

"Very well," said Socrates, "and I am sure, Laches, that you would consider courage to be a very noble quality?"

"Most noble, certainly."

"But what would you say of foolish endurance? Is that not on the other hand to be regarded as hurtful?"

"True," said Laches. "I ought not to say that, Socrates. And is anything noble which is evil and hurtful?"

"Then you would not admit that sort of endurance to be courage?" asked Socrates, "...for it is not noble, but courage is noble."

"You are right," answered Laches.

"Then, according to you, only the wise endurance is courage?"

"True."

Now that courage was expanded to wise endurance, Socrates led Laches through a dialogue to discover what this was. Did courage include a man who remained at his post because his enemy was weaker than he? Was it not more courageous to stay at your post though defeat was imminent? Yes, Laches thought this was so.

"But surely, this is a foolish endurance in comparison with the other," Socrates said.

"That is true."

"And you would say that in a cavalry battle, he who is a good horseman and endures is not so courageous as the man who has no such skill to endure?"

"So I should say."

"And he who dives into a well without any knowledge of diving is more courageous than one who is a skilled diver and dives?"

"Why, Socrates, what else can a man say?"

The Greeks: Socrates, Plato, Aristotle

"And yet men who run such risks and endure are foolish, Laches, in comparison to those who do the same things, having the skill to do them."

"That is true."

"But foolish boldness and endurance appeared before to be evil and hurtful to us."

"Quite true."

"Whereas courage was said to be a noble quality."

"True."

"And now, on the contrary, we are saying that the foolish endurance which we agreed was dishonorable, is courage."

"Very true."

"And we are right in saying so? Can courage be foolish and hurtful and dishonorable?"

"Indeed, Socrates, I am sure that we are not right in saying that," Laches replied.

They ended in a paradox. Laches and Socrates asked how courage could be noble and foolish at once. There was something obviously faulty with Laches' idea of courage. Socrates had helped Laches to reexamine his opinion. The confused General said, "I fancy that I do know the nature of courage, only somehow or other, she has slipped away from me, and I cannot get hold of her and tell her nature." Still, he was closer to perhaps looking at courage for the first time.

This was Socrates' method—an exasperating one to all, but valued by many. He led them into contradiction and paradox, not just to entertain himself, but to awaken them to the confusion of their own thoughts. Those who awoke were grateful. Those who were comfortable in their sleep harbored their anger and grew vindictive.

What right did Socrates have to elicit such confusion? Well, he believed he had a divine duty, **a mission**. Long ago he had had another sign besides the inner voice, the voice which held him back from certain things or caused him to stop in one spot for hours and wonder, but never told him what he should do. This other sign came from the **Oracle of Delphi**. One of Socrates' friends who considered him very wise went to ask the oracle or priestess, if there were any man wiser than Socrates. Now the Oracle of Delphi's information was **enigmatic** in nature. That is, it could be taken in at least two ways—the words were always a mystery to be unraveled. The priestess answered, "There is no man wiser than Socrates." On hearing this, Socrates was at first completely baffled. He had always maintained that he had nothing to teach. He knew nothing.

The Greeks: Socrates, Plato, Aristotle

What could he teach? Therefore, how could he be the wisest? To answer this oracle, he set about to see if he could find a wiser man than he. What he found astonished him.

After much searching and conversation with those who claimed wisdom or who appeared wise, Socrates saw that those who were called wise were indeed ignorant, assuming themselves wise about all subjects because they had received recognition for being wise at one or a few things. The politicians, the professors, the poets—all who claimed wisdom became confused, contradictory, even angry in conversation. Socrates discovered the most lacking were those whose reputation included wisdom. The common man, who knew nothing, was more apt to be receptive when wisdom displayed itself fleetingly in conversation. It appeared that when a man excelled at one thing, he assumed himself to be wise in all things and ceased examination of opinions which controlled his life. Thus the mystery of Delphi was unraveled. There was no man wiser than Socrates. Although a common custom of the day, wisdom was a rare occurrence indeed. Socrates was not so much wise as he was graced with the knowing that he did not know anything. With this advantage he accepted what seemed a divine calling to assist others in unearthing their own contradictions and unmasking the masquerade of wisdom. The man who admits he knows nothing can be seen wisest of all because he is no longer deluding himself. The chance to see what is real is still available.

Socrates maneuvered within this availability. He gave up earning a living in order to devote himself to this pursuit, forsaking all of the comforts and leisure pursuits his contemporaries accepted. He wore the same cloak winter and summer, often going without shoes and eating very simply. His children were destined for such poverty as well. Later, when he was convicted for impiety himself, Socrates defended how he had occupied his days exposing the hollowness of what we call our wisdom. "People suppose I am wise myself in those things in which I accuse another of ignorance. They are mistaken. The god alone is wise, and his Oracle declares that human wisdom is worth little or nothing. That man is wisest who like Socrates knows that he is worthless as far as wisdom is concerned. The disgraceful ignorance is to think you know what you do not know." Somehow his simple existence mirrored a validity beyond words.

But there were many who felt they knew more than they did. The **Sophists** seemed the worst perpetrators of the ignorance Socrates considered a disgrace. Today we call someone a sophist who is glib and cynical, distorting the truth while playing word games. Then it meant a teacher who supposedly possessed wisdom, cleverness, and practical ability. Socrates' definition was closer to ours. He saw them as intentional or misled pretenders of knowledge. Whereas he did not consider himself a teacher and never charged for his discussions, the Sophists placed themselves above others, dispensing their knowledge for a fee. They lectured instead of

The Greeks: Socrates, Plato, Aristotle

offering open dialogue. Socrates disliked them because he believed they distorted the truth and prevented men from pursuing their own thinking. The Sophists had many followers. Crowds would hang on to every word and then repeat them as if they were personally experiencing truths, whether they had understood the words or not. This dismayed Socrates deeply. It was difficult for him to engage them, for their process was one of long-winded discourse in poetic and perfectly phrased, almost hypnotic language. They were not open to Socrates' questions. They were as evil as books, thought Socrates, for one is never allowed to pose the appropriate question at the appropriate time but must wait until the web of words has trapped its victim into believing everything because it sounds as if it makes sense.

After one of these long-winded displays at a dinner party on the subject of poetry, Socrates suggested that they "Leave the poets and keep to ourselves... let us try the mettle of one another and make proof of the truth in conversation." Protagoras, a Sophist, was coaxed to join Socrates but became very uncomfortable with Socrates asking all the questions. So Socrates let him ask the questions. Then Socrates was given his turn. They discussed virtues, beginning with "Are wisdom and temperance and courage and justice and holiness five names for the same thing, or are they each separate things?" Socrates led Protagoras to see the contradictions in his thinking that virtue could be taught to a point where Protagoras could see that it could *not* be taught. For a man who earned his living by teaching virtue, this was too much to bear. Though elenchos had been reached, in Protagoras' disgrace he displayed noble spirit by saying, "I am the last man in the world to be envious. I applaud your energy and your conduct of an argument, Socrates. As I have often said, I admire you above all the men I know, and far above all the men of our own age. And I go further than that. I would not be surprised, Socrates, if you were to become one of the world's famous sages." Even a Sophist had the chance to learn, to change, to be convinced; but all Sophists were not as open or right intentioned as Protagoras.

This was Socrates' relationship to and evaluation of the Sophists. Some were noble of spirit but most were clever, capable, in truth con artists indiscriminately selling artificial food for the soul.

Those attending the Festival of Dionysus and Aristophanes' play *The Clouds* were not aware, however, of just where Socrates stood in relation to the Sophists. The play was a lampoon against all philosophers. Even Aristophanes didn't consider it a serious commentary, just a way of poking fun. But to the audience who saw the play, the mockery that was made of Socrates seemed fair because they knew no differently. The common man went away from the play thinking Socrates a Sophist, which he was not. Aristophanes painted him as a man with both feet off the ground who concerned himself with studying the art of false reasoning and the magnitude of the skies. Though Socrates was well known as a truth seeker in Athens, most people did not know Socrates the man. Aristophanes gave them an image. Even Socrates chuckled at this image. But it was an image eventually harmful to Socrates.

All these occurrences took place against the backdrop of Greece. Socrates had grown up in the **Golden Age,** epitomized by Athens. It was a period of expansion, both intellectually and politically. Athens was the birthplace of **democracy** in a land of aristocrats and **oligarchs**. It was the purest form of democracy in history. Every citizen participated in decisions, or at least was invited to participate. But, as in many developing nations, power struggles began. Athens and Sparta went to war. Socrates was a dutiful soldier and citizen during this period. To his peers he seemed fearless and capable. He watched the wars come, the plagues, the famine, the demoralization of his beloved Athens, the degeneration of justice. He never shunned his responsibilities to the state, nor did he ever evidence anything but heroic commitment. Still, he went about asking his questions, untouched while executions and banishments went on. Yet, at the time when Athens ousted the corrupt politicians who had filled the void after Athens had surrendered to Sparta and was able to rise out of her own degeneracy to pursue democracy and justice and the beautiful, Athens dealt Socrates a strange fate.

Many had watched and speculated, as had Socrates, during the course of war and peace and the collapse of Athens. Those who finally reclaimed their Athens felt someone had to be blamed for the wrong choices which led their city-state to such a demise. Instead of blaming the power mongers who wanted to consolidate other areas under Athenian rule, they blamed the philosophers, especially the Sophists. The Sophists had filled men with so much uncertainty that they fell prey to the men in power, who were the poor or confused choosers. Many of these men had at one time or another befriended Socrates as well as many of the Sophists.

Anytus was one of those men who had watched the crumbling of Athens. He had survived the war, the tyranny, the lawlessness. He, too, blamed the philosophers for stirring things up, for poking fun, for boring holes into the fabric of Athens. Socrates, more than anyone else, disturbed the Athenians, leading them to doubt. Socrates was dangerous. But how could Anytus charge Socrates with just being 'dangerous,' or for merely having known some of those in power who later became tyrants? Athens had no laws against such things. Anytus decided instead to convince a religious fanatic named Meletus to charge Socrates with impiety, for offenses against the gods, and for corrupting the youth.

As plans often will, this one took a turn Anytus did not anticipate. Instead of fleeing as Anytus had hoped he would, Socrates shocked him by deciding to meet the charge. It was a very serious charge, not believing in the gods. Religious feeling was as integral to an Athenian as was patriotism to the politician and in reality were bound one to the other. Those who would judge Socrates would have strong feelings about this issue, would have the memory of a devastated

The Greeks: Socrates, Plato, Aristotle

Athens and their own personal losses. Those who would judge him knew this man from Aristophanes, who years before had tried to show the absurd and sacrilegious nature of this man called Socrates. In order to defend himself, Socrates had first to destroy the image which Aristophanes had created in the minds of those men now to judge him.

It was the year 400 B.C. It was the end of an era where a Golden Age had evolved into one of torment and terror. Never again would they be led into such destruction. Never again would they be so foolish as to allow Socrates in their midst. This was the climate prevailing for the trial. The charge against Socrates was lethal enough, the personal prejudice high, the public mind clouded with fear.

Fearless as always, his conscience the final master, Socrates faced his accusers. It cannot be said that Socrates defended himself. Defense implies some culpability. Rather did he lecture his judges to counter Aristophanes' stereotype, to relate his divine calling and his lifetime of activities as his commitment to it. He told them of the inner voice, how he had given up a comfortable existence, of the Oracle of Delphi, how he had never charged for his services, how indeed he never had considered himself a teacher. If he was not a teacher, how then could he be charged with teaching impiety? Questioning was his activity, not dispensing knowledge. In his own words, "I was never anyone's teacher, so no one was my pupil. I am ready to ask questions of rich and poor alike, and if any man wishes to answer me, and then listen to what I have to say, he may. But I cannot be blamed if those men turn out bad, nor praised if they turn out good, for I never taught or claimed to teach any of them any knowledge whatever."

Perhaps most remarkable, Socrates never threw himself on the mercy of the court, nor did he ever try to 'weasel' out of his charge. Judgment would have to be based on where his conscience had led him, not the details of family, old age, or sentimentality. Thus Socrates committed his cause " . . . to God . . . to be decided as is best for you and for me."

A secret ballot would decide this. Of 501 jurors, the votes tallied found Socrates guilty of the charges by a vote of 281 to 220. Now the punishment would determine the fate of this dangerous subversive.

In Athens the law required one penalty devised by the court and one counterproposal by the defendant. The guilty would naturally choose a lesser punishment than the court. The jury would then decide. Death was Meletus' choice. Most people would then have chosen exile as had Anaxagoras many years before. For many reasons Socrates chose a reward instead of the lesser punishment of exile. He believed he had offered a service and was innocent. To have lesser punishment of exile. He believed he had offered a service and was innocent. To have suggested a punishment, especially exile, would mean he had some guilt. Instead he asked that he be granted free meals for the rest of his life while he continued to go about helping men examine their lives and seeing the confusion of their thoughts. This was, of course, received as a mockery. Socrates knew it would be. He knew also the reaction it would cause. The vote against him was overwhelming. Death was the judgment of the state of Athens.

Without resentment he received this verdict. "Perhaps," he said, "it was right for these things to have happened." But his warning was ominous to his jurors, for Socrates suggested that by killing him they would ensure the immortality of his questions. This meant more to Socrates than his own life; rather, this *was* his life. He was not afraid of dying. His inner voice did not hold him back from it as it had from other ventures many times before. What more was to be said? "The hour of departure has arrived," Socrates declared. "We go our separate ways—I to die and you to live. Which is better is known to God alone." Since he believed that the popular will was not the ultimate test of right and wrong, that an eternal justice existed, Socrates knew his death to be a beginning of the exposure of that justice. Truth was above politics and conscience beyond the law; justice, therefore, lay beyond this trial.

Socrates never wavered, even while awaiting his execution. When his friends confronted him with their questions and plots to escape, Socrates listened compassionately but said merely that considerations of expense, reputation, his children, his wife were to him beside the point. What mattered was that he had pursued his conscience, had let it lead him to this fate. Once he entered the courtroom, he demonstrated a respect for and agreement with the state to trust and abide by its decision. But the agreement was a higher one still. For it was a pact with God. How could a man be virtuous all his life and then evade the very consequences which would define or announce the purpose or destiny for which that life had been intended? All that Socrates had done, all he had helped to expose, would seem ridiculous with an old man afraid to die, clinging greedily to a life which if not lived according to conscience was not worth living.

It was not so easy for his friends and disciples, one of which was Plato. They grieved for the loss of so great a man and even more for what such a fate indicated for the state of mind in Athens. Socrates' last words during his last days eased them some, but their grief was selfish. Who would now go amongst them exposing them to their own selves? They searched Socrates' words for some guidance. "There is a world beyond our world; and, if men could see it, they would know that this other world is the place of the true heaven and the true light and the true earth. Compared to it, our earth, and the stones, and our whole world, are spoiled and rusted, as in the sea where all things are rusted by the brine. Nor is there anything noble or perfect in

The Greeks: Socrates, Plato, Aristotle

our world, but only caverns, and sand, and mud." It is a place, he said, "where . . . everything that grows — trees and flowers and fruits — are fairer than anything here. There are hills whose stones are smoother and lovelier than our highly valued emeralds and jaspers and sardonyxes. And the men of that other world have no disease, and live much longer than we do, and all their senses are far more perfect than ours. And they have temples in which to converse with the gods and hear their voices and receive their answers."

As Robert Silverberg quotes him as saying, " . . . ideas are eternal. A tree might wither, a horse might die, but the idea is perfect and everlasting. Our world, which is only the flickering shadow on the cave wall, can never attain the perfection of the ideal world. No line is ever perfectly straight in our world, no triangle is ever perfectly triangular. We can come close, but perfection is reserved for the ideal world alone." We take it from these words, as did Socrates' friends, that the spirit of Socrates will live though the body die, for the truths he exposed in them, in us, have their perfect and eternal place in the world of ideals.

After these words, after he had taken the hemlock and walked till his legs felt heavy, he lay down. The very last thing he said was, "Crito, I owe a cock to Ascelpious. Will you remember to pay the debt?" Then he covered his own face, stirred slightly, and Socrates, the man, left the world.

As he assured us, his being remains. These last excerpts, communicated 2,377 years later, demonstrate not only Socrates' abstract truths but also the personal man who lived them. Justice and virtue, though ideals, filtered down to each specific act, like repaying a minuscule debt, a strange last concern for a man about to die. But it was not strange. Were this life and death not in accordance with conscience? To have strived for the ideal, though the ideal seem nebulous and unattainable or unpopular amongst men—Socrates reached always for this reality, examining himself, touching his life to the ideal in each concrete, everyday action— even so infinitesimal an action as one man dying.

What then remains to us? The bid, the bid to know one's true self. "We can try," said Socrates. We can strive with all our hearts, and above all with all our minds, to break out of our prison. We can examine our thoughts and struggle to understand the nature of reality, and work to ascend into that higher world of pure ideas. Perhaps that world could not be reached by mortal men; but Socrates said, "Possibly after long struggle we might at least have a brief glimpse into that bright world of truth and perfection," that bright world which is truly our self, shining and free. That Socrates reached for this world, this self, is evident. That he caught his brief glimpse of its light while still amongst us, incredible. That he reaches toward us even now, so many light years away placing that small question before us, a miracle.

Vocabulary

socratic method

dialectic	Oracle of Delphi	impiety
elenchos	enigmatic	paradox
mission	deme	inquiry
sophist	nous	oligarch
method of inquiry	democracy	Golden Age
contradiction	conscience	
soul	a calling	

Greek school of thought: transpersonal domain:

contemplate at separate sittings.

contemplate socrates' life.

contemplate a drawing or sculpture of socrates' face.

wonder about how plato felt about socrates.

contemplate how socrates and plato began aristotle's journey.

during your daily meditation and your insight about your own self, remember socrates' own statement and living of it: "an unexamined life is not worth living."

The Greeks: Socrates, Plato, Aristotle

ACTIVITIES:
COGNITIVE DOMAIN
Knowledge—Comprehension—Application—Analysis—Synthesis—Evaluation

GREEK SCHOOL OF THOUGHT
Knowledge—Cognitive Domain
Describe Socrates' method of conversation.

GREEK SCHOOL OF THOUGHT
Comprehension—Cognitive Domain
Explain how Socrates' method of conversation explored ideas and sought truth.

GREEK SCHOOL OF THOUGHT
Application—Cognitive Domain
Find and document examples of at least five people who display the "disgraceful ignorance" of thinking they know what they do not know. Consider advertisements, commercials, and acquaintances as sources of examples.

GREEK SCHOOL OF THOUGHT
Analysis—Cognitive Domain
Tape-record a class discussion or a conversation. Identify the questions that elicited information and thinking. In what ways is this conversation similar or different from Socrates' method?

GREEK SCHOOL OF THOUGHT
Synthesis—Cognitive Domain
Devise a Socratic conversation on a topic of importance such as drug use, war, poverty, etc.

GREEK SCHOOL OF THOUGHT
Evaluation—Cognitive Domain
Evaluate the effectiveness of the Socratic method for a modern student, based on at least five criteria you develop or choose as important.

The Greeks: Socrates, Plato, Aristotle

AFFECTIVE DOMAIN
Receiving—Responding—Valuing—Organizing—Characterizing

GREEK SCHOOL OF THOUGHT
Receiving—Affective Domain
Listen to the story or a recording of the Death of Socrates.

GREEK SCHOOL OF THOUGHT
Responding —Affective Domain
How do you feel about the way Socrates faced his death? Why do you feel that way? How do you think his judges felt? Why would they feel that way? How might Anytus have felt? Why?

GREEK SCHOOL OF THOUGHT
Valuing—Affective Domain
Draw a line 8" long. At one end, write "disagree" and at the other end write "agree." Put an "X" at the place on the line that indicates how you feel about Socrates' willingness to die for his beliefs. Explain why your "X" is where it is on the line.

GREEK SCHOOL OF THOUGHT
Organizing —Affective Domain
Considering both negative and positive aspects, what do you think Socrates' death accomplished? Explain and provide reasons for your response.

GREEK SCHOOL OF THOUGHT
Characterizing—Affective Domain
In an ideal society, how would people with very different or revolutionary ideas be treated? Explain how such a society or system would work.

BIBLIOGRAPHY

Title: *Greece* (grades 4-6)
Author: Anton Powell
Publisher: Watts, 1987

Title: *The Apology, Crito and Phaedo and the Republic*
Publisher: Available in various paperback editions.

Title: *Plato's Republic*
Author: Plato,
  translated by Benjamin Jowett
Publisher: Airmont, 1968

Title: *Plato Reader*
Author: Ronald B. Levinson
Publisher: Houghton Mifflin, 1967

Title: *Aristotle for Everybody*
Author: Mortimer Adler
Publisher: Bantam Books, 1983

FILMS

The Trial of Socrates
The Death of Socrates
Plato's Apology
The Question
Matter of Conscience

The Greeks: Socrates, Plato, Aristotle

RESOURCES FOR TEACHERS

Title: *Socrates—The Man and His Work*
Author: A. E. Taylor
Publisher: Routledge, Chapman and Hall, 1960

Title: *Plato—The Man and His Work*
Author: A. E. Taylor
Publisher: Routledge, Chapman and Hall, 1960

Title: *Greek Philosophers*
Author: W. K. Guthrie
Publisher: Harper and Row

Title: *Aristotle* (2nd edition)
Author: George Grote
Publisher: Ayer Company Publishers

Title: *The Last Days of Socrates*
Author: Hugh Tredennick
Publisher: Penguin, 1954

Title: *Socrates—An Approach*
Author: Mario Montvori
Publisher: Benjamins North America, 1988

Title: *A History of Western Philosophy: The Classical Mind*
Author: W. T. Jones
Publisher: Harcourt, Brace & World, Inc., 1969

Title: *Aristotle's Vision of Nature*
Author: Frederich J. Woodbridge
Publisher: Greenwood, 1983

Title: *Aristotle: A Contemporary Appreciation*
Author: Henry B. Veatch
Publisher: Indiana University Press, 1974

Title: *Aristotle for Everybody*
Author: Mortimer Adler
Publisher: Bantam, 1983

Title: *Plato and His Contemporaries*
Author: Guy C. Field
Publisher: Haskell, 1974

Title: *Socrates: An Annoted Bibliography*
Author: Luis E. Navia and Ellen L. Katz
Publisher: Garland Publishing, 1988

Henry David Thoreau

do not live in the world,
in distraction and false dreams,
outside the law.

arise and watch.
follow the way joyfully
through this world and beyond.

follow the way of virtue.
follow the way joyfully
through this world and on beyond!

for consider the world---
a bubble, a mirage.
see the world as it is,
and death shall overlook you.

come, consider the world,
a painted chariot for kings,
a trap for fools.
but he who sees goes free.

from: <u>sayings of the buddha</u>

Henry David Thoreau

HENRY DAVID THOREAU (1817-1862)

Henry David Thoreau

Henry David Thoreau lived a life that was, to himself as it was to others, a great and complex adventure. It was a life rooted, ironically, in simplicity. Because of this enigma and the intensity of his life, it is easier to relate the specifics and chronology of his existence than the 'essence' that was and is Thoreau. Since the spirit which is the 'essential' Thoreau is not easily distilled, writings concerning him must immediately encourage the reader to embark on his or her own relationship with him by reading his works. For Thoreau was to himself, first and foremost, a writer.

He was born on July 12, 1817, in Concord, Massachusetts; his life spanned the political careers of both Thomas Jefferson and Abraham Lincoln. In his short life of 45 years, his understanding encompassed the twilight of man through early civilizations of expansion to the present experiment: America, a country yet in constant flux. This rich and incredible perception of **eternity** and his own daily existence synthesized experience and inspired his later writing. Nothing went unexamined by Thoreau. He figuratively, and quite literally, turned over every rock, observing the jewels of nature and the varmints which scattered under the scrutiny of his sudden and penetrating light. Whether in the stream or the city, Thoreau was always looking, watching, observing, and commenting. His description and analysis were beyond accuracy, striking at the core of each subject. In his presence, the wild things of the forest were calm, allowing his entrance. People meeting him either loved or hated him. No one was left unaffected. Thoreau saw people as they actually were. His eyes penetrated their shoddy disguises and saw through their absurd pretenses.

This intensity of person was a quality evidenced in Thoreau's demeanor. Even as a child, though a solitary personality, he lived deeply, close to the earth and close to himself. Growing up in a once prosperous but now poor family, Thoreau contended with the realities of a large extended family of relatives and boarders. The experience provided constant stimulation and interaction, though there was little space one could mark off as one's own. Yet Thoreau created his own. The space grew within him in response not only to his need but as a reflection of the vastness of nature which was his to explore. By his **self-sufficiency**, curiosity, and need, Thoreau investigated this natural world, extending his own inner boundaries in the process. Perhaps these are the roots of his realization that, "In wildness is the preservation of the world." It suggests that man's route to himself is preserved best by his association with the natural. By this alliance much of his roots, the laws of life, could be inferred and lived.

Such thoughts came to him as an adult. His childhood, of which we know much for Thoreau has written down his recollections, demonstrates the seemingly innate inclination and enthusiasm for the natural and simple life.

Henry David Thoreau

Concord, Massachusetts, provided just the environment to foster this life. It was an educated choice, not a romantic escape. While his mother ran the boarding house, his father the grocery or pencil factory, young Thoreau pursued his formal classroom studies. This included a varied reading of adventure and biography, and a meandering exploration around Concord, a place of meadows, ponds, forests, rivers, and, much as Thoreau regretted it, towns. Henry and his brother John preferred investigating the wild places. After their studies, feeding the chickens and turkeys, milking the cows, and hoeing the family's and their individual gardens, they rambled on foot picking berries or wild grapes, tracking Indians, observing birds, and telling stories. Often they would go to the river or pond to fish, swim, explore in their homemade boat, or float lazily watching the zephyrs play with the leaves and clouds. Thoreau let his mind range the universe, the one song. Space and possibilities were limitless here. Returning to his small attic room Henry enshrined this vastness, within himself.

Concord was an abundant setting, with a stream slow enough to drift in but prolific with fish; a place of many moods, of seasons, and of silence. It was a place with a legendary history of peaceful Indian relations. Thus the name, Concord. It marked an agreeable experience in contrast to those of other American towns. It was a place of diverse intellect and spiritual endeavor, close to its natural origins but, in the eyes of Thoreau, with one grave flaw . . . that peculiar institution . . . **civilization**. Hemmed in by its manners and etiquettes to appease its boredom, Thoreau outgrew it early, discarding this ill-fitting suit for nature, especially his own.

A child fascinated with wonder, Henry was often considered self-centered. In the highest sense of this phrase, he was. All **reality** entered and departed through this center, this sense of 'I.' To Thoreau 'I' was the center of the universe; all things moved towards it.

Though seemingly shy, almost too quiet, this outwardly well-behaved boy was a ferocious interpreter both of natural and human realities. Those who knew him well nicknamed him 'the judge.' His discussions and admonishments, which developed early, were good humoredly encouraged by his family. School also helped him to cultivate this. For at the Concord Academy where Henry attended classes, he studied history, logic, Latin, French, and Greek. Another enduring pastime, the flute, he learned here. But as Thoreau himself explains, he actively valued a raw and natural education, pursuing his own interests over a rigid, enclosed study confined to books and a classroom. Though he did extend great value to books, he felt them often misused; rather than leading the reader back to himself, his own concerns, they often led one away. Like Socrates, Thoreau felt books could delay a person's actually thinking and acting for himself. Consistent with this, Thoreau expressed his disappointment in college when he attended Harvard. He felt that its emphasis on the separate branches of knowledge as opposed to their roots or a holistic association of knowledge was ultimately destructive to students.

Henry David Thoreau

Though he studied history, languages, rhetoric, the sciences, it was Thoreau who attempted to associate, to unify past, present, future—eternity—with the daily life, the moment. It was Thoreau who related the separate topics into the one subject, reality. Later when he began teaching at a school of his own design, he attempted to draw learning and life into closer relatedness to the students' needs. Descriptions of his school depict the use of nature and close personal association between student and teacher, often obscuring the line between them. The unique peculiarities of each student were the basis of the curriculum. Integration of subjects, of man and nature, of mind and body, were its guiding principles. Thoreau deplored corporal punishment, rote learning, and severing of the mind from the heart.

Because of some of his opinions, Thoreau's manner often seemed defensive, proud, and antisocial. Indifferent to public opinion, Thoreau often said no more than his peers appreciated or cared to hear. He was always examining the course of the individual and the universal man's life. Most people took his affront personally. Thoreau is often considered one of America's first social psychologists. He criticized humanity's failings and investigated alternatives. He viewed the chief mistake to have occurred when man reached the point of having satisfied the line of basic necessity. Civilization, instead of **culture**, developed at that point.

Thoreau distinguished civilization from culture. His culture was not the culture of random amalgamated experience or archaic and comfortable rituals. It was a culture whose goal was the **truth** and purity of man's place in nature, a nature which after meeting its basic needs pursued those **ideals** or values only the human being can **actualize**, or bring to life by action. Thoreau was familiar with many of these by his association with the Hindus, the Greeks, the Orientals, as well as the ideals of the American Revolution and independence. One had only to look around himself to observe the choice man had made and was still making. Alienated from nature, man was busying himself with acquisition and comfort instead of aligning himself with nature, meeting his needs and pursuing the ideals of human rights, friendship, simple living, and the life of the soul. Man chose instead **materialism**— bigger and better houses, clothes for image not utility, food for the tongue instead of the whole body. Through materialism, acquisitiveness, and exploitation of one another, man had indeed become a hostage of his own desires, perhaps forever **alienated**, or severed, from his true concern.

Sometimes Thoreau's choice to take the hard road meant having many odd jobs to get by. He tutored Emerson's children. He surveyed land, did carpentry work, and made pencils, becoming soon a jack-of-all-trades with time enough to pursue his thoughts and interests. But he was not alone in his scathing condemnation of man's alienation from his true nature. Concord's homes and surrounding areas were as abounding with bright minds as its streams

Henry David Thoreau

were with the shining fish Thoreau had caught in his youth. Thoreau associated now with people like the Emersons, the Alcotts, Channing, Sanborn, Fuller, and John Brown, netting a catch of thoughts remarkable and diverse. These people met often in their **Lyceum** group, a group of people who presented and attended various lectures on a variety of subjects, many of which were **metaphysical**. Most of these considered themselves **Transcendentalists**, which meant they transcended or rose above basic needs and concerns, once they had been met, to pursue spiritual ideals. Transcendentalism, popular especially today, was a body of belief with multiple cultural, religious and historical influences. Thoreau and the Transcendentalists believed basically in the infinity of man's spirit, and that God comprises man and the universe. Because man played a special role in this relationship, these people as men and women lived by inspiration, that is, within or toward the original spirit, conducting their lives in harmony with the natural and spiritual laws they were able to discern. It was not a systematic belief, but one of constant discovery and attention to the natural and spiritual realities over the pursuit of individual greed and security characterized by civilization.

But it is really in Thoreau's everyday life, of which his writings, particularly *Walden*, are a reflection, that we see his meanings. It is here that one discovers the 'essential' Thoreau. In *Walden* Thoreau introduces his disapproval of man's current existence and describes his exercise in how a man might live.

Though most people believe Thoreau went to Walden Pond to write *Walden*, he did not. Concerned about the ways of the world, he went to see if he could force life into a corner, to see where the line of necessity could be drawn: just what did a man need to shelter, clothe, and feed himself? Once this was established, the person could attend to this joyfully, learning how to do for himself: bake bread, plant a garden, build a house. This was the beginning of freedom. Then one could turn his energy from improving these conditions to exploring and developing a condition of appreciation for life itself, his own and the vaster life set within. This is *Walden*.

Thoreau begins by explaining his dissatisfactions with civilized life, the echoes of which our youth and our mentally ill resound today. Then he describes his adventures in discovering and attending to the necessities of man's physical life. Later he sets out to rediscover, to appreciate, to value, to comprehend this life, this moment. What he discovers, besides those enduring values all the masters remind us of, is personal, is the center of the web of life man inherits at birth but experiences only as an individual. Thoreau became that individual. His observations and connections are unique. They are science at its highest but transcend science itself. *Walden* is an experience few men have ever had. Among other things, Thoreau discovered that "this curious world which we inhabit is more wonderful than it is convenient; more beautiful than

Henry David Thoreau

it is useful, it is more to be admired and enjoyed than used." And, because he believed God had not sent him into this world without some 'spending money,' Thoreau believed man's consciousness a great gift leaving him ". . . rich in what he can afford to let alone."

Even in reading *Walden* one suspects the story within the story—which is its secret. In reading *Walden* even the reader is anxious and ready to throw off the darkness which prevents the book from becoming the way of the world. After *Walden* even the reader, as Thoreau did always, leans toward beginnings. As has been said of *Walden*, it was ". . . a magnificent attempt to make Thoreau's fellow men understand and appreciate the full possibilities of daily existence." He failed "because he was generally unreceived," but he left behind a book of rules that shows men how to live rich without being rich.

But *Walden* was only one of Thoreau's deep involvements. He concerned himself also with human rights, **civil disobedience**, and a **life of principle**. Set in the context of this Source Guide particularly, Thoreau is in good company. Thoreau's essays on these issues are jewel-like in their observations and logic. They are the creation of a man whose physical life draws the line of necessity, allowing his soul to realize and support the values which only human conscience can. Since Thoreau saw the world as a stage for this drama of man and nature and spirit on earth via the individual, a culture which denies this discovery is alienated from reality, from life itself. Thoreau rejected such a civilization. Once he had realized his conscience and his own heart he could no longer support a government which allowed slavery, denied the individual pursuit of his inner life, or fostered relationships based on exploitation, profit, and materialism. Thoreau spoke out often. Because he was an **abolitionist**, one who supports the end of slavery, it was the issue of slavery which forced his public stand. Though he was ridiculed, jailed, and unreceived by the public, still his words persisted. In "Civil Disobedience," he reminds us:

> . . . government itself, which is only the mode which the people have chosen to execute their will, is equally liable to be abused and perverted before the people can act through it . . . I ask for, not at once no government, but **at once a better government**. Let every man but make known what kind of government would command his respect, and that will be one step toward obtaining it . . . The mass of men serve the state thus, not as men mainly but as machines, with their bodies, . . . In most cases there is no free exercise whatever . . . Why has every man a conscience, then? I think that we should be men first, and **subjects afterward**. It is not desirable to cultivate a respect for the law, so much as for the right. The only obligation which I have a right to assume is to do at any time what I think right . . . I cannot for an instance recognize that political **organization as my** government which is the *slave's* government also . . . an individual, must do justice, cost what it may. If I have unjustly wrested a plank from a drowning man, I must restore it to him though I drown myself . . .

> Action from principle, the perception and performance of right, changes things and relations; it is essentially revolutionary, and does not consist wholly with anything which was. It not only divides states and churches, it divides families; aye, it divides the *individual*, separating the diabolical in him from the divine.

In these startling words as well as in Walden we can see the remnant spirits of the Buddha, and of Socrates, for Thoreau followed a path consistent with them, asking and answering the same questions. Later in this book we will see these remnants reappear in Gandhi, Carson, and King.

Though Thoreau met his life and his death with an intense submission to that 'eternal and cosmical' design, a part of him was disheartened. Had anyone even heard him? Only his faith assured him that the voice which spoke through his small life was a voice audible perhaps to some of us in another time and place. We know now that some have heard.

The 'essential' Thoreau included, then, all his many voices, his many roles. In his life he was a writer, a philosopher, a naturalist, a psychologist, our first **ecologist** and conservationist, a journalist, a surveyor, a dendrologist, a phrenologist, a builder of houses, a hoer of beans, a walker in the morning sun. Above all, an ordinary man. He conversed with men considered long dead but whose spirits he lived for, enriching Thoreau's individual spirit—spirits that spoke to Gandhi, to Carson, to King, and to us. This had been Thoreau's highest Transcendentalist hope. It is hard to deny that his spirit and that of the others persist still. Paper and pen and our ability to read bring them to fuller life, but that the heart recognizes and greets them with understanding and longing is a spontaneous act which precedes these tools by which we communicate.

Thoreau believed this. Therefore, as many before him and since, he did not fear his physical death. He had seen his choice, had chosen, had lived it. The last entry in his journal was on November 3, 1861. A few weeks before, he said to a friend, "I suppose that I have not many months to live; but of course, I know nothing about it. I may add that I am enjoying existence as much as ever, and regret nothing." On May 6, 1862 Thoreau left us, but left to us... that which was the 'essential' Thoreau.

Though Thoreau had thrown off Emerson's paternal cultivation of him, Emerson's eulogy is a rendering of Henry seen through the eyes with which he so desperately sought to merge— the other.

"He knew how to sit immovable, a part of the rock he rested on, until the bird, the reptile, the fish which had retired from him should come back and resume its habits, nay, moved by curiosity, should come to him and watch him.

"It was a pleasure and a privilege to walk with him. He knew the country like a fox or a bird, and passed through it as freely by paths of his own. He knew every track in the snow or on the ground, and what creature had taken this path before him . . . He thought, that, if waked up from a trance . . . he could tell by the plants what time of the year it was within two days.

"The country knows not yet . . . how great a son it has lost. It seems an injury that he should leave in the midst of his broken task, which none else can finish,—a kind of indignity to so noble a soul, that it should depart out of Nature before yet he was really shown to his peers for what he is. But he, at least is content. His soul was made for the noblest society; he had in a short life exhausted the capabilities of this world; wherever there is knowledge, wherever there is virture, wherever there is beauty, he will find a home."

When attempting to hold still for a moment the essence of such another, particularly that seemingly rare breed we refer to as philosopher, it is sometimes enlightening to recollect his last words. With Thoreau they are an ironic yet accurate summation of his life. When asked by his mother whether he had made his peace with God, he answered simply and kindly that, indeed, he ". . . was not aware that we had ever quarreled." In deed and in thought, they had not.

Vocabulary

civil disobedience	life of principle	abolitionist
transcendentalist	alienation	culture
reality	civilization	actualize
self-sufficiency	lyceum	truth
eternity	ideals	metaphysical
	ecologist	materialism

Thoreau: Transpersonal Domain:

contemplate at separate sittings.

meditate while you walk.

contemplate Thoreau's life.

contemplate a picture or sketch of Thoreau.

wonder about the connection between Socrates and Thoreau.

notice the pace of modern life and its effect on you.

During your daily meditation and your resulting insights about your own self, remember Thoreau's love and perceptions of nature and leisure.

ACTIVITIES:
COGNITIVE DOMAIN
Knowledge—Comprehension—Application—Analysis—Synthesis—Evaluation

THOREAU
Knowledge—Cognitive Domain
Relate the story of Thoreau's childhood.

THOREAU
Comprehension—Cognitive Domain
Explain why Thoreau was considered self-centered when he was a child.

THOREAU
Application —Cognitive Domain
Demonstrate how Thoreau's views on slavery could or could not have been predicted from his life and beliefs.

THOREAU
Analysis —Cognitive Domain
Compare and contrast the beliefs of Siddhartha, Socrates and Thoreau.

THOREAU
Synthesis—Cognitive Domain
With a friend, role-play a situation in which Thoreau is talking to a friend who owns several slaves.

THOREAU
Evaluation—Cognitive Domain
Evaluate Thoreau's beliefs that books can delay a person's thinking and acting for him/herself. In what ways is this true? Not true? Why?

THOREAU
Knowledge—Cognitive Domain
Recall what Thoreau said about civilization and man's fault in working away his life.

THOREAU
Comprehension—Cognitive Domain
Explain what Thoreau saw as the difference between civilization and culture.

THOREAU
Application—Cognitive Domain
If you were to choose to live as Thoreau did, how would your life change? Why would each change occur/be made?

THOREAU
Analysis—Cognitive Domain
List 15 elements of your life: include items relating to your home, school, community, and your use of time. Categorize each item as either "necessity" or "luxury." Be able to support each categorization with your own reasoning.

THOREAU
Synthesis—Cognitive Domain
Predict what Thoreau would say in a speech to a national Sierra Club convention. Support each point with evidence.

Henry David Thoreau

THOREAU
Evaluation—Cognitive Domain
Which of the philosophers you know of has led the most meaningful life? Explain what you believe a meaningful life is and why you named the philosopher you did rather than one of the others.

AFFECTIVE DOMAIN
Receiving—Responding—Valuing—Organizing—Characterizing

THOREAU
Receiving—Affective Domain
Listen to parts of a reading of Thoreau's *Walden*, one about nature or seasons.

THOREAU
Responding—Affective Domain
Express your feelings or what you visualized when listening to *Walden* through a poem, painting, collage, or other art form.

THOREAU
Valuing—Affective Domain
Choose at least 5 things you believe Thoreau valued. Rate each one of these things from 1 to 10, with 10 being a very high value, for Thoreau and for yourself. Explain the reasons for all the similarities and the differences between your personal ratings and Thoreau's.

THOREAU
Organizing—Affective Domain
In what ways, if any, might *Walden* be different if it were written today? Explain the reasons for your response.

THOREAU
Characterizing—Affective Domain
If a person were to live today as Thoreau advocated, what would that person's life be like? Make up a person—doctor, lawyer, nurse, teacher, business person, waitress, etc.—and describe his or her daily life.

THOREAU
Receiving—Affective Domain
Take a walk in the woods or a park or your neighborhood.

THOREAU
Responding—Affective Domain
Record what you observe, feel, and sense on the walk.

THOREAU
Valuing—Affective Domain
Decide how important parks and natural environments are to you. Share this information with a friend or group, providing at least three reasons for the importance you designate.

THOREAU
Organizing—Affective Domain
How does the loss of a "non-essential" species change life for humans in general? Why is this so?

THOREAU
Characterizing—Affective Domain
How much of a community should be set aside for parks or natural environmental areas? Design a community that includes such space as well as housing, businesses, schools, and cultural and recreational facilities.

BIBLIOGRAPHY

Title: *Walden and Civil Disobedience* (grades 9-12)
Author: Henry David Thoreau, Edited by Owen Thomas
Publisher: Norton, 1966

Title: *Henry David Thoreau*
Author: Introduction by Harold Bloom
Publisher: Chelsea House, 1987

Title: *Walden with Reader's Guide* (grades 7-12)
Author: Henry David Thoreau
Publisher: AMSCO School Publications, 1973

Title: *Henry David Thoreau's Walden: Modern Interpretations*
Author: Edited by Harold Bloom
Publisher: Chelsea House, 1987

Title: *Walden* (grades 7-12)
Author: Henry David Thoreau
Publisher: AMSCO School Publications, 1969

Title: *Henry David Thoreau: Writer and Rebel*
Author: Philip Van Doren Stern
Publisher: T. Y. Crowell Co., 1972

Title: *The Night Thoreau Spent in Jail*
Author: Jerome Lawrence and Robert E. Lee
Publisher: Bantam Books, 1982

Henry David Thoreau

FILMS
Living Earth
Leaf
Seeing Eye

ALBUMS
Narration of Walden
Environments: Sounds of the Stream and Forest

RESOURCES FOR TEACHERS

Title: *Walden and Civil Disobedience* (Annoted)
Author: Edited by Owen Thomas
Publisher: Norton, 1966

Title: *Walden and Other Writings*
Author: Henry David Thoreau
Edited by Brooks Atkinson
Publisher: McGraw Hill, 1981

Title: *In Wildness is the Preservation of the World* (Good introduction)
Author: Selections and Photos by Eliot Porter
Publisher: Sierra Club–Ballantine Books, 1988

Title: *Thoreau: On Man and Nature*
Author: Henry David Thoreau
Publisher: Peter Pauper

Title: *Thoreau: Mystic, Prophet, Ecologist*
Author: William Wolf
Publisher: United Church, 1974

Title: *Thoreau Stalks the Land Disguised as a Father*
Author: Barry Targan
Publisher: Greenfield Rev. Press, 1975

Title: *The Senses of Walden*
Author: Stanley Cavell
Publisher: North Point Press, 1981

Title: *Thoreau: A Naturalist's Liberty*
Author: John Hildebidle
Publisher: Harvard University Press, 1983

Title: *Henry David Thoreau*
Author: Leon Edel
Publisher: University of Minnesota Press, 1970

Title: *Henry Thoreau as Remembered by a Young Friend*
Author: Edward W. Emerson
Publisher: Thoreau Fund, 1968

Title: *The Shores of America: Thoreau's Inward Exploration*
Author: Sherman Paul
Publisher: Books Demand, UMI, 1989

Title: *Emerson and Thoreau: Transcendentalists in Conflict*
Author: Joel Porte
Publisher: AMS Press, 1980

Title: *The Influence of Thoreau's Civil Disobedience on Gandhi's Satyagraha*
Author: George Henrich
Publisher: New England Quarterly, 1956. XXIX, 462-471

Mohandas K. Gandhi

Few cross over the river.
Most are stranded on this side.
On the riverbank they run up and down.
But the wise man, following the way,
crosses over, beyond the reach of death.
He leaves the dark way
for the way of light.
He leaves his home, seeking
happiness on the hard road.
Free from desire,
free from possesions,
free from the dark recesses of the heart.
Free from attachment and appetite,
following the seven lights of awakening,
and rejoicing greatly in his freedom,
in this world the wise man
becomes himself a light,
pure, shining, free.

         from: <u>Sayings of the Buddha</u>

Mohandas K. Gandhi

Mohandas K. Gandhi (1869-1947)

Mohandas K. Gandhi

Mohandas K. Gandhi—man of paradox, man of truth. Perhaps it is an even greater paradox that so great a soul, a **mahatma**, was brought forth in a world which at the same time birthed and nurtured Adolf Hitler. The ancient quest for self, for truth, for life, though seemingly severed in these two answers, accomplished at last a living and obvious choice.

Though it would take him years to realize and accept his path, and the rest of his life to confront its magnitude, confusions, and consequences, the child in Gandhi was father to the man. Born in the coastal town of Porbandar on October 2, 1869, Mohandas met a city of diverse and unresolved religious and political communities. Generally, though, all were far removed from the spirit of the long forgotten Golden Age in India. Few but the highest caste of priests had any direct realization of the Indian culture they shared or the original inspirations which distinguished their values. Most preferred to seek fulfillment in human economics and fraternity. It was not an environment to revive a sense of the past, eternity, truth, or beauty. Though Porbandar was eyecatching in its temples and pinnacles, the business and insecurities encompassed the city as if in a haze. Self-seeking fulfillment through action in society had reached a kind of blindness.

British imperialism had invaded India. This bustle of society, this blindness, this loss of their individual connection to culture and values made most Indians controllable, useful, and, ironically, grateful. The British benefits of economics and authority were accepted as if by an ignorant but trusting child.

Gandhi's family reflected this state of mind. Being neither uneducated nor of high sophistication, they were members of the sub-caste Bania, meaning businessmen. Gandhi's father, Kaba, was the premier of Porbandar; he served as an official under the British political agent for that area. The family lived in a subdivided three-story building around a courtyard where the environment was communal, that is, shared with extended family, and moderate in its economy and advantages.

The Gandhis practiced **Hinduism**, a religion which worships **Vishnu** as the incarnation of the absolute truth. Vishnu exemplified a path similar to the Buddha, that truth is the foundation of the world and of human life. Morality was based then on truth, on one's consciousness of it. Putlibai, Gandhi's mother, was a devout, relaxed, and joyful Hindu. Though Gandhi was educated in the basic tenets and stories of Hinduism, and exposed to its celebrations and rituals, it was his mother's piety and living common sense which Gandhi admits was his religious influence.

Not unlike other boys, Gandhi experimented with the many pranks and forbiddens. Prohibitions against smoking, alcohol, profanity, theft, and, because they were **vegetarian**, meat, were common Hindu restraints. Gandhi was tempted by all these. He spent his adolescence confronting them: his conscience and his distaste of lies, sneaking about, and secrecy. Gandhi the man viewed this period as a natural and useful stage, a kind of negative education. It was the beginning of his alignment with truth over the lie. Though he contended with these all his life, his awareness of their pitfalls developed early.

Education during these years was fairly uneventful. Gandhi was an average student, but he remembered only once or twice the delight in actually grasping a truth, theorem, or idea for the first time. Even though he later became the son chosen for special education, Gandhi did not feel it was his scholastic achievement which merited this.

Marriage for most Hindus seems premature to Westerners. Gandhi himself later agreed with this, but at the age of 13 it was exciting, chaotic, and self-consuming. School, his wife, Kasturbai, and his furtive and prankish escapades exhausted Gandhi by 16 as one is at 20. Though there were sporadic and traditionally arranged separations from his wife, Gandhi attended to little else. To his grief, his passions even preoccupied him the night his father lay dying. Gandhi long regretted not being allowed to share those last moments. The shame was a constant reminder of his desires and self-possession.

This shame grew in Gandhi, as did his desires. He felt surely that a man should be able to subdue his passions in order to live a more human and rounded life. He even tried to teach Kasturbai, to cultivate her mind. By age 19 he needed to escape. He needed a change, a chance to find himself. It was decided by his family that he would be the son to receive an education and pursue a career. After much thought and professional and religious counsel, a career and schooling were decided upon. Gandhi was convinced that he should become a lawyer. To do so he had to travel to England to study. Though it was very painful to leave his young wife and son, a heavy burden was lifted. Gandhi dreamt of more than escape, he dreamt of England—"the land of the philosophers and poets, the very center of civilization." There was much opposition on the part of his caste and religion. It was believed that a Hindu could hardly remain pure among such pagan-intellectualism, and meat-eaters at that. Gandhi's mother found these fears contagious and wavered on her permission. Finally, after much counsel and discussion, Gandhi took a vow not to participate in those sacrilegious activities he had sometimes himself committed. Thus on September 4, 1888, at age 19 Gandhi embarked for Bombay en route to his final destination—London.

Mohandas K. Gandhi

At this stage of his life Gandhi was, admittedly, immature, terribly shy, awkward, and ineffectual. He trembled before audiences or had others read his papers. Now, in a foreign culture, he could not even leave his room. Not only was he normally embarrassed by himself, but he was doubly embarrassed at his ignorance and inability to fit into the posh sophistication of London. Accepting Britain as a superior culture, he was embarrassed at his inferiority to it. Gandhi was impressed easily. His disenchantment with the British would happen many years hence.

During his stay in England, Gandhi eventually did mingle. At first it was with his classmates. Later it was with the people in general. But because he had taken his vows, his vegetarianism and inability to date women held him back. He seemed less attractive by these restraints, and many would not bother with him or else tried to reform him, especially the Christians. But soon he found his company to keep. At first his vegetarianism was a block to social relatedness. Then it become its cornerstone. Through friends he found some vegetarian restaurants and some books by Westerners supporting and exploring the purposes and methods of such a diet. Through this he was led to the Theosophical Society, a group of people pursuing world enlightenment through education, diet, and action. Their motto was: "There is no religion higher than truth."

During these years and this exposure Gandhi was also to explore much ancient and contemporary literature. The list is seemingly endless, but many are particularly interesting: Buddha, Socrates, the Bible, the Koran, Kipling, Tennyson, Shelley, Lenin, Buber, Emerson, Krishna, the **Bhagavad Gita**, the Upanishads, Tagore, Bentham, and interestingly enough Henry David Thoreau and Tolstoy. Later, partly because of this avenue opening, he chose to rediscover his own religion, Hinduism, to study it, realize it, and criticize it.

Through this Gandhi gained a world and historical perspective—his socialization and his first glimpse of the absolute truth. He also discovered his inner teacher and the kingdom within himself. Perhaps a key concept in his later beliefs was initiated here, that of **dharma, duty, vocation**, what a person is for. As Geoffrey Ashe discusses the Bhagavad Gita:

> This is bound up with the caste theory: Arjuna is a warrior-noble and has responsibilities which he must not evade, whatever his feelings. But the lesson is more profound than the theory. Krishna's point is that mere emotion—desire, revulsion, pity, even when seemingly praiseworthy—should never divert a man from the central truth of his nature. You are what you are, you must find out what you are called to do in the world's scheme, and you must do it without brooding over the consequences. The frets and lusts of the individual self are liars. Krishna tells

called to do in the world's scheme, and you must do it without brooding over the consequences. The frets and lusts of the individual self are liars. Krishna tells Arjuna to conquer this petty self, and enter into the higher Selfhood of . . . Truth through ardent devotion and disinterested action in keeping with his own calling.

Gandhi's means to realizing and actualizing, that is, discovering and living his dharma, was to become, unconsciously at first, the path of karma yoga, salvation through action. He was to become one of this century's revivalists of that path. This decision was perhaps a result of the transpersonal, transcultural connections he made during his explorations. Not only did he read in his own language, but he reread English interpretations and reinterpreted them into his own life and beliefs. Ashe writes: "He was discovering his own heritage through a Westerner, who focused it and made sense of it as Indians themselves did not." He did this again and again with other texts, but especially the Bhagavad Gita. He partially described it himself in a letter written some years later when he was reading Emerson: "The essays to my mind contain the teaching of Indian wisdom in a Western guru. It is interesting to see our own sometimes thus differently fashioned." In his London phase it was more than interesting—it was decisive.

When it came time to return home in 1891, Gandhi had indeed accomplished his original and conscious task of becoming a lawyer. But his unconscious mission, the acquisition of thought and spirit, had become part of him as well. Though not an obvious baggage the day he landed, India's chosen son had come home. He was still the immature, shy, and ineffectual boy who had left, but the beginnings of the man to come could be seen in his ability to relate his knowledge as one integral whole, connecting one at first to personal issues and consequently to one's national and universal beliefs.

Gandhi's career led him from India to South Africa. In South Africa he confronted his own inadequacies again, inadequacies he had always run from before. It was here that conscious choice in his **transformation** began. He had a difficult case to solve over a family corporate disagreement. Emotion was high. Gandhi was unfamiliar with the languages, customs, and values. Overcoming his fear daily, he studied, he contemplated, he drew upon all he had learned, and he asked for guidance. And he received it. Through this case he discovered the basis for law.

> "When I was making preparation for Dada Abdulla's case, I had not fully realized the paramount importance of facts. Facts mean truth, and once we adhere to truth, the law comes to our aid naturally . . . My job was boundless. I had learned the true practice of law. I had learned to find out the better side of human nature and to enter

men's hearts. I realized that the true function of a lawyer was to unite parties riven asunder. The lesson was so indelibly burnt into me that a large part of my time during the twenty years of my practice as a lawyer was occupied in bringing about private compromises of hundreds of cases. I lost nothing thereby—not even money, certainly not my soul."

It was in Africa that Gandhi also experienced extremes of prejudice against himself. It was here that he stood up against this prejudice for truth. His sympathy for the poor and oppressed of his country, the **untouchables**, for the untouchables in all countries, began in Africa. He confronted his own greed, the hollowness of trying to appear European and the loss of his own cultural dreams and values. He saw clearly the never-ending complications of a household dedicated to impressing and maintaining social status. When Kasturbai and their two sons joined him, the inconsistencies and confusion mounted. Slowly he and his family began the path of **brahmacharya**, self-control, discipline, and **self-reliance**. They began by doing more things for and by themselves—including pressing their own clothes and reassuming their traditional garments and customs of simplicity. In his marriage, his daily life, and his career he began to align himself more with necessity and truth. He attended to his duty as a husband, a lawyer, a citizen, rather than always doggedly pursuing his own rights. Duty precedes requests for rights, he thought. Rights will follow naturally if duty is upheld. If they do not, then one's duty will lead one rightfully to claiming one's rights even at the expense of disobedience and noncooperation.

Thus began Gandhi's transformation. His **conversion** from a self-seeking, timid person to a self-pursuing duty and the absolute truth in all things via conscience ensued. This path, his dharma or duty, became one of self-chosen disciplines and abstentions from food, sex, and comforts; therefore, his self-reliance was born. The way was cleared.

This was the developing point of view. In South Africa it meant much prejudice and, as he began representing Indians there, he became politically unpopular. In response to ridicule, the obstacles, discrimination, and eventual violence, Gandhi realized a technique parallel to his emerging self-control, self-reliance, and conscience of right and wrong: nonviolent noncooperation. Along with these self-revelations he also accepted these three maxims:

- That the good of the individual is contained in the good of all.
- That a lawyer's work has the same value as the barber's, inasmuch as all have the same right of earning their livelihood from their work.

- That a life of labor, i.e., the life of the tiller of soil and the handicraftsman, is a life no less worthy of living than one of high rank.

This was a marked divergence from his traditional Hindu belief in the caste system. Because of this divergence, Gandhi moved freely among all classes. Because of it, he came to revere even the lives cast out as untouchable.

These revelations and empathy for all people, for life, for truth, were a compatible match to spark nonviolence into action and political machinery.

Influenced by Tolstoy's *The Kindgom of God is Within You* and Thoreau's essays "A Life Without Principle" and "Civil Disobedience," Gandhi found his conscience and sense of truth within himself. He understood then that if a man's conscience could discern a wrong he must point it out and resist it. Simply stated, his technique was based on **ahimsa**, love and nonviolence in all forms of thought, word, and action. He felt that once one sees, touches, and appreciates his own life, his own kingdom, all life becomes valid and revered. Violence is a denial of validity. From Thoreau he received well thought out and described explanations and methods, methods which became more pronounced and effective when he contained them in his **satyagraha**. When he returned to India they would prove invincible in his demands for Home Rule, a demand which later became one for complete independence from England.

Gandhi took then this vow of nonviolence and required it of his associates and followers, even when met with violence. He believed that the correct action or reply to evil was correct insight that one needed to first reach through meditation and correct understanding of what was right and wrong. To achieve this one needed to see one's own violence and its roots in fear, pride, greed, and ambition. One had to observe and cultivate nonviolence of the mind, ridding the self of hate, prejudice, and passion. One must seek the truth in all moments, then, the spirit of life which is love. As Geoffrey Ashe has so magnificently outlined, nonviolence, the path of satyagraha or **'truth-force,'** is:

> At the heart of the situation, however, obscured by myth or propaganda ... truth. It is not only truth-in-this-instance but Truth with a capital T. In achieving his correct insight the Satyagraha encounters the Absolute. That encounter supplies his marching orders. "Here," he says, "is the point of no return and no appeal. Here I must stand, I can no other." The hackneyed phrase 'the Moment of Truth' is in this case apt.

> Having won through to a reality free from illusion, he draws strength from the meeting. Gandhi ... after his fashion ... saw it as a meeting with God. Talking in 1931

to the Swiss pacifist Pierre Ceresole, he sketched his belief as it had then matured: "Truth is God, and the way to find him is nonviolence. Anger must be banished, and fear and falsehood. You must lose yourself . . . Purified, you get power. It's not your own, it's God's."

When Truth shines unclouded before him, the Satyagraha asserts it by a fearless refusal to submit to the Wrong or co-operate with it. This usually involves public acts of dissent and disobedience, and may extend to setting up new institutions, political or economic. He keeps to his nonviolence, not only on moral grounds but so as to hold firm in his own mind. To allow violence to possess him would be to lose his correct insight, and slip back through hatred into error. ("In war," as has been observed, "Truth is the first casualty.") Nonviolence means a clean break with the normal habits of mankind, a rebirth into light.

This became Gandhi's satyagraha, or holding to the truth. It was to become a method of a nation's struggles for independence, a battle of love and truth against hate and the lie. Many were freed, not only from the external devils of foreign rule, but from the inner demons of ignorance, fear, greed, and violence.

More specifically, the methods by which Gandhi achieved this on a personal plane included meditation, inner transformation, constant observation of Truth—of his own fear, conditioning, and pride—days of fast, self-control over indulgence, restrictions of passions, spiritual study, solitary walks, reductions of material comforts—thus dependencies—and joy. The methods employed on the political plane were as described by Ashe:

> Satyagrahi, Gandhi decided, can employ such weapons as boycotts and strikes. But when authority moves against them they must submit to its blows without retaliation, and go to prison, or responsibility falls on each one, as soldiers of nonviolence. Satyagraha implies self-reliance, not raising of committees. It calls for colossal self-control.

> The Satyagrahi—in theory—not only consents to suffer at the wrongdoer's hands, but conquers through suffering. Martyrdom is part of the method. In his agony he is driven back on the unwavering divine Truth at the center of his soul, and that contact makes him invincible. Yet his victory is not the opponent's defeat. It is the opponent's **conversion**. To endure blows long enough to unnerve the arm that strikes them, and win over the directing mind. Victory does not mean that one side triumphs at the other's expense, but that both sides are reconciled in a new harmony, with the Wrong cancelled.

Mohandas K. Gandhi

The chronology and magnitude of the details by which this occurred, the actual **boycotts**, dissent, disobedience, the **dhurnas** or sit-down strikes, and the actual incidents of the Salt March, the Spinning Wheel, and the independence and concurrent secession of Pakistan comprise a history too lengthy to contain in so short a sketch. Needless to say, an extended biography of Ghandi is recommended to the reader to fully comprehend and appreciate this complicated, changing man, this funny-looking, cheerful, childlike **bapu**, or father.

Then and now he has been a great **guru** or teacher, but always he sends us back to our own inner teacher—the moment and our conscience. He reminds us of the brotherhood of man, of the garment of God, and of one's duty, hence salvation. He recites from the Upanishads, "The whole world is the garment of God. Renounce it then, and receive it back as the gift of God."

Many, like Martin Luther King, Jr., have since interpreted and made their own Gandhi's wisdom, innocence, and karmic duty. In a world still divided by fear, hate, greed, and misunderstanding, the enlightened and simple love he counseled is not the balm of banality warning man to control his passions or perish; it is one man's living example shining across time and space and culture, promising us that which we all seek—the gift of self-containment and reliance, a rich life to live, and a unified planet within which to celebrate.

On January 30, 1948, a Hindu fanatic who misunderstood and disagreed with Gandhi's nonviolence towards Pakistan and the Muslims knelt before him, bowed, and fired three shots into Gandhi's heart. Gandhi's last words were: "**Rama**, Rama, Rama!" The assassin replied, "In the name of God, I forgive you, I love you, I bless you." Gandhi lived and died not by the presence or absence of that God but by its possibility.

Very little remained physically or materially of Gandhi after his burial—two pairs of sandals, some eating and cooking utensils, his writing tools, his glasses, a few small books, his pocketwatch, his prayer beads, and his ashes. Shining and free, his spirit was released.

As Albert Einstein, a man of magnitude in his own way, so beautifully and simply eulogized Gandhi, "Generations to come, it may be, will scarce believe that such a one as this ever in flesh and blood walked upon this earth."

Vocabulary

mahatma	vocation	dharma
hinduism	ahimsa	bhagavad gita
karma yoga	Vishnu	transformation
satyagraha	bapu	untouchables
self-reliance	dhurna	brahmacharya
conversion	rama	absolute
vegetarian	guru	'truth-force'
	duty	boycott

Gandhi: Transpersonal Domain:
Contemplate at separate sittings.

Contemplate your own violence, what causes this reaction? Fear, pride, greed?

Contemplate and observe non-violence of the mind.

Contemplate and observe what is right and wrong in your own conscience, do you stand up to it when your conscience tells you to? Why not?

Contemplate Gandhi's life. What was his message?

Contemplate a sketch or portrait or picture of Gandhi's face.

Contemplate one incident in Gandhi's life or transformation.

During your daily meditation and resulting insights about your own self, remember Gandhi's life. How does your life realize or deny what he discovered? During Gandhi's meditation he used the words Rama, Rama, Rama, to help him to let go of thoughts.

Mohandas K. Gandhi

ACTIVITIES:
COGNITIVE DOMAIN
Knowledge—Comprehension—Application—Analysis—Synthesis—Evaluation

MOHANDAS K. GANDHI
Knowledge—Cognitive Domain
Recall Gandhi's explanation of nonviolence, ahimsa.

MOHANDAS K. GANDHI
Comprehension—Cognitive Domain
Explain the reasons, goals, and methods of ahimsa.

MOHANDAS K. GANDHI
Application—Cognitive Domain
Dramatize an incident from the news with potential or actual violence and how nonviolence could be used in that instance.

MOHANDAS K. GANDHI
Analysis —Cognitive Domain
Analyze, diagram, or make a flow chart illustrating how a violent reaction is different from a response of nonviolence. What is the karma or effect of violence and nonviolence?

MOHANDAS K. GANDHI
Synthesis—Cognitive Domain
Project what might have happened if one or more of the leaders at the time of a (historical) war had chosen the course of nonviolence. What would have been the major immediate and long-term effects of the nonviolence?

MOHANDAS K. GANDHI
Evaluation—Cognitive Domain
Evaluate violence and nonviolence for resolving conflicts. Consider effectiveness and personal and general gain or damage. Give specific examples to illustrate your points.

MOHANDAS K. GANDHI
Knowledge—Cognitive Domain
Briefly tell a friend or the class about Gandhi's life and death.

MOHANDAS K. GANDHI
Comprehension—Cognitive Domain
Describe what happened at the time of Gandhi's death and how he responded. Why did he respond in this way?

MOHANDAS K. GANDHI
Application—Cognitive Domain
Explain how Gandhi's death utterance was consistent with his beliefs and his life.

MOHANDAS K. GANDHI
Analysis—Cognitive Domain
Compare the beliefs and thinking of a fanatic such as the one who killed Ghandi to those of Gandhi himself. What similarities and differences exist between them?

MOHANDAS K. GANDHI
Synthesis—Cognitive Domain
If Gandhi had lived out his natural life span, what do you think he might have accomplished? Why would he have accomplished those things?

MOHANDAS K. GANDHI
Evaluation—Cognitive Domain
Evaluate Gandhi's life in terms of the changes he effected. Decide how important he was in the history of India and why he was or was not of importance.

AFFECTIVE DOMAIN
Receiving—Responding—Valuing—Organizing—Characterizing

MOHANDAS K. GANDHI
Receiving—Affective Domain
Contemplate Gandhi's life and death.

MOHANDAS K. GANDHI
Responding—Affective Domain
Compose a eulogy for Gandhi based on your contemplation of his life.

MOHANDAS K. GANDHI
Valuing —Affective Domain
Poll ten people and ask them to rate Gandhi's influence and importance on a scale of 1 to 10. Record each person's reasons for the rating they gave. Make a chart of the ratings and the reasons; include your own.

MOHANDAS K. GANDHI
Organizing —Affective Domain
Explain how Gandhi's values affected his life, in his youth and in maturity. Name values he held, actions related to these values, and the reasons for the actions.

MOHANDAS K. GANDHI
Characterizing—Affective Domain
Describe a day in the life of your family if you all lived according to Gandhi's principles. Explain why the day would be the way you describe it.

MOHANDAS K. GANDHI
Receiving—Affective Domain
Contemplate, read, or listen to a story about Gandhi's transformation from a shy, bungling, fearful, and incompetent person to a self-assured leader of millions.

Mohandas K. Gandhi

MOHANDAS K. GANDHI
Responding—Affective Domain
In what ways do you identify with Ghandi's characteristics, either as a youth or as an adult? Explain why this is so.

MOHANDAS K. GANDHI
Valuing—Affective Domain
Who do you believe was most important to the society he/she lived in—Gandhi, Rachel Carson, or Martin Luther King, Jr.? Why do you believe this?

MOHANDAS K. GANDHI
Organizing—Affective Domain
What personal values caused Gandhi to change from an "exciting, chaotic, and self-consuming life," to one of self-denial and meditation? Explain the relationship between his personal values and his behavior.

MOHANDAS K. GANDHI
Characterizing—Affective Domain
If Gandhi were to be the teacher in your classroom for one month, what would school be like for you? Give reasons for your statements.

BIBLIOGRAPHY

Title: *Gandhi* (grades 4-8)
Author: Nigel Hunter
Publisher: Bookwright Press, 1987

Title: *Gandhi* (Grades 7-10)
Author: Patricia Bahree
Publisher: David and Charles, Batsford, England, 1989

Title: *Gandhi—The Man*
Author: Eknath Easwaran
Publisher: Nilgiri Press, 1978

Title: *An Autobiography—The Story of My Experiments with Truth*
Author: Mohandas K. Gandhi
Publisher: Dover, 1983

FILMS

Gandhi
I Am Also You
The Brotherhood of Man

MUSIC
Indian Ragas

RESOURCES FOR TEACHERS

Title: *Autobiography—The Story of My Experiences with Truth*
Author: Mohandas K. Gandhi
Publisher: Dover, 1983

Title: *Mahatma Gandhi and His Apostles*
Author: Ved Mehta
Publisher: Penguin, 1977

Title: *Gandhi: His Relevance for Our Times*
Author: Edited by Ramachandran and Mahadeven
Publisher: Greenleaf Books, 1983

Title: *Gandhi on Non-Violence: Selected Texts from Gandhi's Non-Violence in Peace and War*
Author: Edited by Thomas Merton
Publisher: New Directions, 1965

Title: *Gandhi's Truth: On the Origins of Militant Non-Violence*
Author: Erik Erikson
Publisher: Norton, 1970

Title: *Gandhi as a Political Strategist: with Essays on Ethics and Politics*
Author: Gene Sharp
Publisher: Porter Sargent, 1979

Title: *Gandhi and Civil Disobedience*
Author: Amar K. Singh
Publisher: Longwood Publishing Group, 1980

Title: *Gandhi* (Excellent)
Author: Geoffrey Ashe
Publisher: Scarborough House, 1969

Title: *Gandhi Remembered*
Author: Horace Alexander
Publisher: Pendle Hill, 1969

Title: *Philosophy of Mahatma Gandhi*
Author: Dhirendra Datta
Publisher: University of Wisconsin Press, 1953

Title: *Gandhi Reader: A Sourcebook of His Life and Writings*
Author: Edited by Homer Jack
Publisher: Grove, 1989

Title: *Life of Mahatma Gandhi*
Author: Louis Fisher
Publisher: Harper & Row, 1983

Mohandas K. Gandhi

Title: *All Men are Brothers: Life and Thoughts of Mahatma Gandhi as Told in His Own Words*
Author: Mahatma Gandhi
Publisher: Continuum

Title: *The Assassination of Mahatma Gandhi*
Author: K. L. Gauba
Publisher: InterCulture, 1969

Title: *Gandhi and the Contemporary World: Studies in Peace and War*
Author: Edited by Misra and Gangal
Publisher: South Asia Books, 1982

Title: *Gandhi—The Man*
Author: Eknath Easwaran
Publisher: Nilgri Press, 1978

Title: *Mahatma*
Author: D. H. Tendulkar, Volume 2
Publisher: Greenleaf Books, 1983

Title: *The Mind of Mahatma Ghandi*
Author: Edited by R. K. Prabhu and U.R. Rao
Publisher: Greenleaf Books, 1988

seeker!
do not be reckless.
meditate constantly.
or you will swallow fire
and cry out: "no more!"

if you are not wise,
how can you steady the mind?
if you cannot quieten yourself,
what will you ever learn?

how will you become free?

with a quiet mind
come into that empty house, your heart,
and feel the joy of the way
beyond the world.

      Look within---
      the rising and the falling.
      what happiness!
      how sweet to be free!

      it is the beginning of life,
      of mastery and patience,
      of good friends along the way,
      of a pure and active life.

      from:
      sayings of the buddha

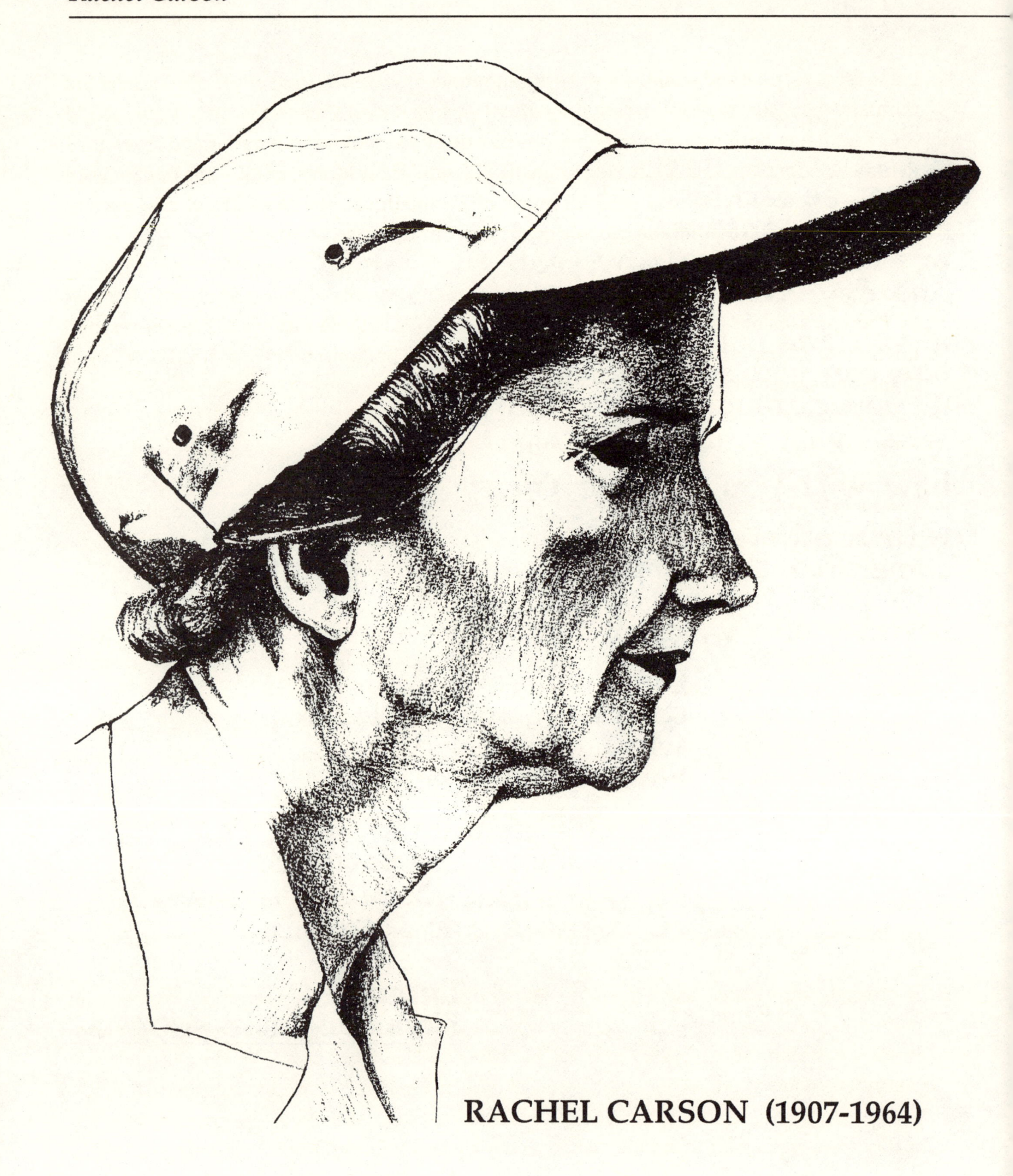

Rachel Carson

RACHEL CARSON (1907-1964)

For most of us, poet and scientist are at opposite ends of the **continuum**, two unique modes but mutually exclusive ways of perceiving natural events. Rachel Carson disproved this, as did Thoreau. Being both poet and scientist, she blended knowledge and **wonder** and love into a delicate wisdom. She could hold the moment still, until the minutest detail—the opening of a milkweed pod, the pure and ethereal music of a whitethroat, the orchestra of crickets and cicadas—took on a magnitude capable of shaking our universe, at least for a time.

Rachel was by no means a romanticist. Her observations, insights, and descriptions, influenced by Thoreau's vision, were sensitive and accurate, unifying with the heart of all life. She reached this level of reality via the rigors of formal education, exploration, and experience, but brought to this an essence uniquely Rachel.

From childhood she developed within and from this essence, naturally yearning to know and explore the 50 acres of land around her home. Her mother and father always supported her enthusiasm for the outdoors, but presented the world in many ways: poetry, nature walks, accurate texts, and much sharing. It was a close family filled with respect for nature and for the natures of one another.

Born in Springdale, Pennsylvania, in 1907, the youngest by eight years of three children, Rachel grew up in a varied and natural environment encompassed in love. Within this environment, she could foster her dreams and excitements. She decided at 7 to be a writer and began submitting her stories and essays at 11. Mostly she dealt with her own experiences, just sharing her thoughts about real events. One of her first stories concerned an English pilot killed in an accident while helping to train our pilots during World War I. It was difficult for Rachel to comprehend the inequities of war. No matter how she tried, she just could not understand it, especially how they spoiled her dreams of the sea. Her mother would read poems of the sea before Rachel went to bed at night. Rachel would then go off to bed holding her head quite still so as not to shake loose the thoughts of the sea. But during the war her dreams saw the submarines, the torpedoes, and the death of men, fish, and even the great rolling solemnity.

In order to forget the sea she immersed herself in school and outdoor exploration. A motivated student, Rachel excelled in all she studied except science, but especially English. She was encouraged to go to college by parents and teachers but discouraged by the reality of her family's economic situation. A scholarship was her only chance. She applied for a full scholarship to Pennsylvania College for Women. Everyone said she had a good chance, but reality answered again with $100, hardly enough even for books. But her parents so believed

Rachel Carson

in her potential that they went into debt to secure her education. Rachel loved college, involving herself in many activities but most resolutely in her writing. Towards her junior year she realized she had to take some science to fulfill her requirements for graduation. She dreaded the boring lab work but resigned herself to the necessity of it. The vocabulary would be the toughest, she thought, but she could probably manage to stay awake in class. It was a biology class taught by Miss Mary Skinner.

The class would change Rachel's path radically and align her with what was to become her ultimate concern—life. After the first day, Rachel came out of class shocked at herself and amazed. She had never quite appreciated science that way, always remembering it as dry and disconnected from what was real for her. But here was a teacher who preserved the wonder, who gave facts a context of beauty and her own joy of being alive. Rachel eventually changed her major, against much teacher and parental objection, from English to **marine zoology**, the study of the sea. Rachel had found another life—hers. This was a new science, she thought. This was what had been missing—a wonder and a reverence for the intricacies of nature. Not a nature to assault with microscope and thought alone, but a world to be perceived with all the senses of being—smell, touch, vision, hearing, taste, wonder—all the subtleties of consciousness a narrow science cannot recognize but a wider science can intuit.

Rachel spent her last year immersed in science, astounding those who had once admonished her by graduating **magna cum laude**—with great honor. She won a full scholarship to Johns Hopkins University and a six-week study tour at Woods Hole on Cape Cod aboard a marine biology research vessel. The ship's purpose was to study the life of the sea. Rachel was the only woman aboard, surrounded by famous American scientists, and her yearning for the sea found its resolution. She had never even seen the ocean. She was overwhelmed more by the sea and its vast and prolific mysteries than by the great honor being paid her.

While on the cruise Rachel met many influential people. Several worked for the Bureau of Fisheries, which later became the Department of Fish and Wildlife. She asked about the possibility of getting a job some day. The answer she received was to become a familiar hurdle, a common prejudice: "We don't have women" working here. Someone did give her a name to contact, though, along with an incredulous grin. When she returned to school in the fall, she went to see this Mr. Higgins at the Bureau and was told again that there was no place for women.

Rachel's time was consumed then with school and exploration in her field, so much so that this disappointment did not dominate her. Two part-time jobs kept her quite occupied, and there was also much to worry about. The stock market crashed, leaving her family and her unable to maintain two households. Moving back together resolved a good deal of this and the camaraderie lifted everyone's spirit. But this was only the first of several **traumas** to erupt in Rachel's life. Papa died suddenly in 1935. Rachel had to make some money. She braced herself and went again to see Mr. Higgins. A surprise met her. There was a job, not for a woman, but for a scientist who could write. Rachel was the only one so far who could qualify.

Seven-minute short stories about fish was the assignment. They were to be radio broadcasts sponsored by the Bureau. Later they would be published in one volume. As with all other endeavors, Rachel became deeply involved, often writing and rewriting till the sun rose and the dawn's chorus began. Mr. Higgins was very pleased. He had been unable to find a scientist who could write or a writer who understood science. Here was a person who excelled in and blended the two with remarkable style and sensitivity.

While fulfilling this job, Rachel learned of yet another job opening at the Bureau. It was for a Junior **Aquatic Biologist**. An aquatic biologist would have to possess a knowledge of both river and sea to qualify. Rachel studied. Amongst 1,000 applicants Rachel was the only woman taking the test. Her mother encouraged her. She believed Rachel would qualify. Rachel wasn't sure. As if in a dream, Rachel remembered standing in front of Mr. Higgins' desk, as incredulous as he, to learn that she had been accepted for the position of Junior Aquatic Biologist with the top score of 1,000 applicants. She worked as biologist during the day answering questions and researching what she couldn't answer. It meant many long trips to the libraries and being indoors, but the money was a necessity, especially as other incidents intervened. At night Rachel worked on the "Fish Tales," her own writing.

Another trauma and two more mouths to feed: Rachel's widowed sister died, leaving two school-age girls. Rachel raised them as her own. Now money became of prime concern. She began writing articles but time was always a factor. Although her mother surprised her by learning to type at 70 years of age, there was just too much for even two people to do. A rejected introduction for the "Fish Tales" anthology was later accepted by The Atlantic magazine. But this money dwindled fast. Many famous scientists and writers also began to encourage her to write a book. Thus began her real writing career. But how to get time, and where to get money if she simply took the time? Eventually, after much struggle through three jobs, the book was

Rachel Carson

miraculously published and became a best-seller. *Under the Sea Wind* was released in 1941 and captured the public's eye for about one month. Then World War II darkened all enthusiasm.

Rachel watched another war even more confused than when she was a child, for now her understanding and appreciation of the world was tenfold. She wept again for the men, for the sea, for life. She studied the discoveries of the sea as they came across her desk. When they were available for public release, Rachel would include her new knowledge of the sea in her next tribute to nature.

By 1948, Rachel was Editor-in-Chief, directing five people including men. It was not often now that people mistook her for a messenger girl at the Bureau. She was busy with her next book, becoming known and respected as both scientist and writer. But she was very tired. A literary agent was hired to do the footwork and public relations, which eased the burden. Rachel just couldn't get the time to write what she wanted to write. Even when she took off from work there was double the work when she returned. Yet her writing was being well received. *Yale Review* paid her a $1,000 prize; she was selling parts of her next book to various magazines; *Reader's Digest* offered her $10,000 to condense the books. But nothing was giving her the freedom to write. Finally, a grant came from the Guggenheim Fund for $4,000. Rachel took a year off with no deadline. *The Sea Around Us* was published in July 1952 and by December was selling 4,000 copies a day. It was on the best-seller list—as was *Under The Sea Wind*, reprinted after 11 years. Rachel now had two best-sellers at the same time. It was a glorious tribute, not so much to herself but to the sea and the earth, a primal alliance. People responded to her sense of reality and yearned for this perception to prevail amongst the intelligent world, if indeed after two devastating wars it still existed.

For a while fame monopolized her time. She met this graciously, and her natural shyness developed into a reserved but capable public face. Fame did not change Rachel. She saw it as a chance to educate even more people and viewed this as an honor paid more to life than to her.

At this time, yet another shock invaded Rachel's already hectic life. One of the two girls she had raised who was widowed and raising her own child, had died suddenly, leaving Rachel a five-year-old boy. Rachel now had a son named Roger. She took him with her as much as possible, sharing her sense of wonder and love for the world around them. Roger became a grateful tagalong like the young Rachel of many years ago had been to her older brother, Roger. He rekindled Rachel's own sense of awe and together they discovered and rediscovered the minute and vast mysteries of the earth and sea.

Now Rachel had enough time and money to do nothing but write, and she intended to do just that. She turned down all other offers so that she could write the book she had hoped all her life to write, a book that would take her at least five years to write. The sense of wonder and the invulnerable, immeasurable perfection of this planet was her theme. Love was her purpose. Rachel understood the many magnificent **ecologies** of the one, the delicate weave of all living things in the competition for space and food and light to which even man must succumb. Rachel wanted time to appreciate this, to comprehend this, to preserve it in her writings so that others could share in her wonder, in its wonder. Her understanding gathered now into an empathy and guardianship. Later this awareness of the interconnected web of plant, insect, animal, and man amplified her alarm.

Rachel's purpose was focused now towards confronting the reality which threatened that theme. She received letters in 1958 concerning **DDT**, an insecticide being used to rid crops of insects. There are many dangers inherent in its use. Traces of it pass through the food chain, resulting in deaths and genetic alterations as well as producing strains of insects which eventually reproduce a breed immune to the **pesticide**. Songbirds were dying daily then from minute traces left in the bugs they ate, who had eaten the plants upon which was the residue DDT. After writing letters to all parts of the world, Rachel realized that she was in the best position to help. The alarm was critical and she took the challenge as a painful but necessary duty of conscience. Mama vowed to help but died suddenly that December. Rachel's main supporter, especially during this loneliest of vigils, was gone. Rachel floundered but life kindled her devotion to the work ahead.

Rachel never wanted to write a book such as *Silent Spring*. Like Thoreau she had an ominous duty to recognize and warn man to this deadly crossroads. Ironically, she had to harvest in her **prophecy** the fruits Thoreau had once alluded to in his condemnation of man's relationship not only to one another but to life itself. His statements concerning man's abuse and exploitation of nature were little heeded in his time. They were little heeded when Rachel described the results or karma which had ensued since Thoreau's time. He had known not the specifics or the timetable; perhaps he had hoped someone like him, like Rachel, would in speaking out offer humans another chance, a chance not just to look, but to see. Rachel saw in writing and research that she had to confront and admit that man was capable of destroying this natural order which she met so joyfully each day. Invulnerable as she had always believed the planet to be, Rachel now saw the eventual results of man's exploitation and interference, especially with insecticides, accruing.

Rachel Carson

The book of oracles was Rachel's last. About the same time she undertook the battle against one disease she developed another: cancer. She told everyone it was arthritis and worked to the finish on *Silent Spring*, publishing in 1962 a book which shook the entire globe. The large companies and many newspapers ridiculed it and attempted to darken her name, but truth and understanding shone in her words. The earth stood by her. Rachel had won a battle for the world she both understood and loved, but she left us amid this danger one spring day in 1964.

Considering all the gifts that Rachel gave, with all the burdens of being human she lifted to her with love and joy, it is a sad return we have given her to allow the death of so much life encompassed in doubt as to the world's future. *Silent Spring* was her last word. The book expressed a strange kind of wonder at a stranger kind of occurrence by man, a natural being destroying his natural and only home with his innate intelligence turned against himself. Keats helped her find that last word, but the meaning rings as ominous today as it did then, as

> the sedge is withered from the lake
> and no birds sing.

Vocabulary

ecology
marine zoology
DDT
magna cum laude

trauma
wonder
pesticides

prophecy
continuum
aquatic biologist

Rachel Carson:
transpersonal domain:

contemplate at separate sittings.

contemplate Rachel's love of the sea.

contemplate Rachel's love of nature and her sense of wonder.

contemplate Rachel's life, and her eventual mission to expose d.d.t.

contemplate a sketch or photograph of Rachel.

during your daily meditation and your resulting insights about your own self, remember Rachel's life and her wonder, how does your life realize or deny this existence?

Rachel Carson

ACTIVITIES:
COGNITIVE DOMAIN
Knowledge—Comprehension—Application—Analysis—Synthesis—Evaluation

RACHEL CARSON
Knowledge—Cognitive Domain
List all of the books Rachel Carson wrote.

RACHEL CARSON
Comprehension—Cognitive Domain
Explain briefly the subject of Rachel Carson's books.

RACHEL CARSON
Application—Cognitive Domain
What effect do you think Rachel Carson's fascination with the sea had on her view of and concern for the whole planet? Explain your reasons.

RACHEL CARSON
Analysis—Cognitive Domain
Compare the reception by the public of two of Rachel Carson's books. Explain the reasons for the similarities and differences you find.

RACHEL CARSON
Synthesis—Cognitive Domain
Develop a visual, audio, or written presentation that combines media and that would attract people to read one or more of Rachel Carson's books.

RACHEL CARSON
Evaluation—Cognitive Domain
Select the book by Rachel Carson that has been the most important to humankind. Provide at least five reasons to support your choice.

RACHEL CARSON
Knowledge—Cognitive Domain
List some of the hardships in Rachel Carson's life.

RACHEL CARSON
Comprehension—Cognitive Domain
Explain how each hardship Rachel Carson suffered may have helped and/or hindered her.

RACHEL CARSON
Application—Cognitive Domain
Dramatize Rachel Carson's reactions to some of the adversity in her life.

RACHEL CARSON
Analysis—Cognitive Domain
Compare Rachel Carson's life with Gandhi's. What similarities and differences do you find and what effects did these have?

RACHEL CARSON
Synthesis—Cognitive Domain
Compose a poem highlighting the ups and downs in Rachel Carson's life.

RACHEL CARSON
Evaluation—Cognitive Domain
Compare two of the hardships in Rachel Carson's life and choose which one had the most impact. Explain why you believe as you do.

AFFECTIVE DOMAIN
Receiving—Responding—Valuing—Organizing—Characterizing

RACHEL CARSON
Receiving—Affective Domain
Visit the sea, the desert, a forest, or a beautiful garden with no intent other than to receive it.

RACHEL CARSON
Responding—Affective Domain
Express through art, music, dance, poetry, or other means your response to the visit.

RACHEL CARSON
Valuing—Affective Domain
List five of your recent experiences, including the visit to a natural environment. Rank these in order of their importance to you. Explain your ranking.

RACHEL CARSON
Organizing—Affective Domain
With another person, develop a list of natural resources, in order of their importance. Both persons must reach agreement on the order and be able to provide reasons.

RACHEL CARSON
Characterizing—Affective Domain
Rachel Carson loved the sea even before she saw it. What holds a fascination for you even though you have not seen or experienced it? What in your life or personality may have caused this fascination?

RACHEL CARSON
Receiving —Affective Domain
Listen to "La Mer."

RACHEL CARSON
Responding—Affective Domain
Using the medium of your choice, express your response to "La Mer."

RACHEL CARSON
Valuing—Affective Domain
Relate and listen to your own and others' responses to "La Mer." Who seemed to get the most out of "La Mer"? Why do you think that is so?

Rachel Carson

RACHEL CARSON
Organizing—Affective Domain
How important are music and art to our appreciation of the environment? Assign a value of 1 to 5 to their importance and explain your reasons for the rating.

RACHEL CARSON
Characterizing—Affective Domain
Think about science and art: how they are related and what each contributes to our lives. Using any means or media you choose, express this relationship and value.

BIBLIOGRAPHY

Title: *Rachel Carson: Who Loved the Sea* (grades 2-5)
Author: Jean Lee Latham
Publisher: Garrard Publishing Co., 1973

Title: *The Sense of Wonder*
Author: Rachel Carson
Publisher: Harper & Row, 1987

Title: *Rachel Carson: Pioneer of Ecology* (grades 2-7)
Author: Kathleen Kudlinski
Publisher: Penguin, 1988

Title: *The Sea Around Us*
Author: Rachel Carson
Publisher: Oxford University Press, 1989

BOOKS BY RACHEL CARSON
(grades 8 & up)
The Sea Around Us
The Edge of the Sea
Under the Sea Wind
Silent Spring

FILMS
The Silent Spring of Rachel Carson
A Source of Wonder

MUSIC
"La Mer," by Debussy
"Environments: Ocean"
"The Moldau," by Smetana
"Ebb Tide," by Earl Grant
"Water Music Suite," by Handel

RESOURCES FOR TEACHERS

Title: *The House of Life—Rachel Carson at Work*
Author: Paul Brooks
Publisher: Houghton, Mifflin, 1989

BOOKS by RACHEL CARSON
The Sea Around Us
The Edge of the Sea
Under the Sea Wind
Silent Spring
The Sense of Wonder

Martin Luther King, Jr.

"look how he abused me and beat me,
how he threw me down and robbed me."
live with such thoughts and you live in hate.

"look how he abused me and beat me,
how he threw me down and robbed me."
abandon such thoughts, and live in love.

    in this world
    hate never dispelled hate.
    only love dispels hate.
    this is the law,
    ancient and inexhaustible.

    you too shall pass away.
    knowing this, how can you quarrel.

    from: <u>sayings of the buddha</u>

Martin Luther King, Jr.

MARTIN LUTHER KING, JR. (1929-1968)

Martin Luther King, Jr.

In another time, in another place, a young man listens to some lectures. He borrows some books. The man: Martin Luther King, Jr. The influences: Henry David Thoreau and Mahatma Gandhi. The questions and understanding Martin brought to those meetings, however, grew from a personal and formal education vast beyond his years. He merely picked up these keys, turned them one at a time, and opened a door allowing over 22 million people to enter, claiming selfhood and citizenry as their birthright.

The education brought to that door was education in the highest sense. For all that is good, worthy, and true in human nature was drawn from within, turning out into the world an ordinary man who simply followed his conscience choice by choice even to his final physical fate—assassination. It was a process of synthesis associating the inheritance of slavery, the personal experience with America's caste system—more commonly called **segregation**—, a loving family, a brutal South, a life rooted in the simple truths of Jesus. Formal education included an early graduation with honors from high school and an early entrance into college. Martin progressed through Morehouse, an all-Negro college in Atlanta. He entered Crozer Theological Seminary in Pennsylvania in 1948 at age 19. This meant being one of six Negroes in a student body of 100. By Martin's third term, he was elected student body president. Martin studied English, literature, sociology, philosophy, and religion. Consistent with his namesake, Martin Luther of the 1500s, he came early to the understanding evidenced in the other Martin's words: " . . . to go against conscience is neither right nor safe. God help me. Amen." With this insight and with awards and scholarships, he enrolled at Boston University to study further his chosen concerns.

Though formal education was a noticeable creative influence in developing Martin's spirit, it was his childhood and adolescence rather than formal studies that provided the central purpose and understanding which he later integrated and shaped.

Born in 1929 in Atlanta, Georgia, a city rebuilt after the shatters of war, Martin, Jr., entered a minister's family, a comparatively comfortable existence, as the second child, the first son. It was a home filled with the realities of Christ's message, a home which fostered individuality, fairness, and love. Martin's father, Martin Luther King, Sr., had grown up as a **sharecropper**. He had lived a hard life subject to extreme poverty and **discrimination**. As a minister and as a person, he refused to accept 'the system' which set aside one part of the democracy, reneging on the Negroes' constitutional rights as persons and citizens. He lived his life and his paternity consistent with these ideals, fostering this respect for and guardianship of the assumption of selfhood and of their African and American heritage.

Martin Luther King, Jr.

Martin witnessed this **commitment**, benefiting from the freedom to grow which it provided. He observed also his father's resistance to being treated as less than a man, whether buying shoes, eating at a lunch counter, or walking down a street. An early reformer, one of the founders of the **NAACP**, the National Association for the Advancement of Colored People, Martin Luther King, Sr., was a model of that which he took as his first assumption—an individual.

Where Martin's father was a persistent, sometimes angry **crusader**, Martin's mother was always calm, persevering, and loving. Her warmth and hope provided balance both for the man Martin Luther King, Sr., and the soon to become a man, Martin, Jr. Martin was closely yet freely bound to both his mother and his grandmother. Grandmother provided an enduring faith in God and a wisdom which encompassed a history few could remember. Along with her daughter, she kept alive for Martin the specifics and emotions of his African ancestry. When Martin began to sense at seven the 'wall' of **prejudice**, that his place in the world was confined by his color, both of these women provided an understanding of the historical pieces which created this, lessening the personal affront. Still Martin wondered at this complicated puzzle of human nature. While Martin puzzled, his father demonstrated the individuality and courage to resist what the heart and mind could understand but knew to be unjust.

Beyond these personal influences, Martin was an average boy filled with all the mischief and curiosities of childhood. His life was full of play, of singing, and of words. An early fascination with the word as an inspiring and powerful tool was encouraged by his family. Silence and quiet times were also provided and valued by the Kings. Martin spent the silence just sitting and thinking or reading the many books made available to him. In books, friendships, and adventures, success and knowledge knew no boundaries of color. Because he never assumed himself any less a person, this vicarious experience developed him further. His mind roamed the world. His heart was affected by the stories of the many selves he encountered.

His mind and heart concerned themselves with the real stories around him as well. Martin wondered at the poverty, the disease, the deformed selves, just as had Buddha, just as had Gandhi. He saw what the system had manifested amongst his people. His heart held the sadness. His mind searched and waited for the way.

Amid this central concern were woven the details of existence, the small junctures of experience which led to the resolve that some day he and his people would be free, that perhaps the human mind itself would break its boundaries. One incident which became a turning point occurred when Martin was in high school. He was on a bus coming home after a public-speaking contest in Valdosta, Georgia. Martin had won second prize. The bus ride was sparked by elation and group pride.

It was the 1940s, and Martin knew well the custom, the laws. Negroes sat at the rear of the bus. If they were sitting near the front and a white person boarded, they automatically moved to the rear. Martin sat up front this day, gaily conversing about the contest. The bus became crowded but Martin did not move. The driver yelled for him to move to the back. Martin did not acknowledge him. The driver began yelling obscenities and threatened to call the police. Martin felt this treatment unfair, regardless of custom or law or his fear. His teacher became concerned at the driver's mounting violence, urging Martin to move. Reluctantly, Martin stood up and moved to the rear. He stood the whole 100 miles remaining in the ride. He vowed then that he would never accept this. He would defeat this. He longed only for an appeal.

This came gradually, though naturally, wholly. The incidents to emerge then occurred spontaneously but haphazardly at first. During college Martin read Plato and Aristotle. He read Thoreau and the Communist doctrine. From Plato and Aristotle, incorporated with the teachings of Christ, he committed his life to the being of the soul, directing the mind through emotion, even through reason, towards the highest ideals, towards truth. From Thoreau he gathered his first politics of nonviolence, of true Christian morality. From Communism he saw the vacuity of such a system founded in materialism only, rather than in the soul, in God. Yet he rejected a Christianity which ignored the economic and social needs of its people. His heart and mind sifted through the rubble and the achievements of civilization. Finally he met the answer. The messenger: Mahatma Gandhi.

Martin's mind was perhaps ripened all his life just for this meeting. Through personal and intellectual experience, he had distinguished the forces of good and evil, of light and dark in the world. He knew the forces were a necessary and unavoidable tension. He knew also that to become an individual, to affect the world, we cannot sit on the fence of indecision; we must commit ourselves one way or the other. Only the heart knows which force we are inherently aligned with. Martin knew his heart. All of the small detours ran headlong now toward this **crossroads**. Martin took this final step into his heart and his choice was made. He stood in a place where Buddha, as well as Socrates and Thoreau and Gandhi and Rachel, had stood. Each in a different life had entered finally that which holds all life and knows no separations.

Martin Luther King, Jr.

To understand this choice, a choice which was just a beginning, we need to remember Gandhi's message and then examine Martin's interpretation and the use of it as a political and moral medium.

Gandhi, also familiar with Socrates, Aristotle, Buddha, and Thoreau, used civil disobedience as a method of satyagraha, truth-force or firmness in the good cause. Civil disobedience is basically nonviolent noncooperation. It is the friction Thoreau had in mind to stall the machinery of an archaic and unjust government. One first aligns oneself with the truth, the ideal, the good cause, using that as the 'force' rather than the force of violence. Gandhi led a nation to independence via methods consistent with satyagraha. He held that truth, that which we know is true in our heart, our conscience, not our intellect, will lead us eventually into conflict with an unjust government whose force emanates from the motives of profit and power, needing the force of violence to embody and convince. The truth-force needs nothing other than itself. Noncooperation is just an obvious result, for how could you know what is right and just in your heart and cooperate with its demise?

Rather than react with violence to protect our rights and the truth, Gandhi said that we must simply refuse to cooperate. We boycott. We do not obey unjust laws. Though the state will react with violence, a person following the way of satyagraha never responds with violence, only **passive resistance**. People following this way have stepped into their hearts, knowing the eternal justice to outlive even their personal lives. Though the consequences may mean imprisonment, injury, even death, when aligned with truth the soul presides, the body endures, the cause will justify itself. Sooner or later truth will win. People will understand with the heart what they could not understand with the mind. Everyone is unavoidably connected, created equal, and worthy of a fair chance for livelihood, happiness, and independence. But more, the person knows that he or she has come into life by making this choice. Gandhi's noncooperation affected the British economically, socially, and morally. For thousands made this choice with him. The whole world watched and applauded their eventual success, mourning Gandhi's assassination as it had no other.

Martin was overwhelmed with love, respect, and the 'way.' He saw the parallel between India's untouchables which Gandhi helped to enlighten and free and America's disinherited blacks. They had been robbed not only of their individual selfhood, but also of their participation in the process of government. Martin knew this to be wrong. Aligning himself with the truth-force he began developing his ideals and ideas of nonviolent resistance, ideas which would unavoidably alter history.

During this time Coretta Scott also entered his life. She brought to him the balance, the intimacy, the personal involvement with life that marriage at its highest meaning can bring. It was 1952. Throughout their courtship and eventual marriage she talked with him. She listened and shared his interests. She shared hers, particularly her music. Coretta contributed a joy and a liveliness which were to constantly replenish Martin's enthusiasm and concern for life. They had four children who added a playfulness and spark which further humanized Martin. Though they learned to share him with the world, Coretta and the children were a touchstone that made Martin's dream more real. The structure and environment of the home were encompassed by values consistent with satyagraha at the personal level. Each moment in his public and personal life, which was one life, became now a medium to learn and more closely align his soul with what was true, right, and just.

Martin and his family lived at first in Montgomery, Alabama. He had begun a ministry at Dexter Avenue Baptist Church, two blocks from the Alabama capitol. It had been a much deliberated choice, whether to return to the South, but once it was chosen both Martin and Coretta knew it was the right choice. Martin could not turn his back on the struggle now.

It was the year 1954. The United States Supreme Court had just rescinded the old **separate-but-equal** doctrine, which maintained the essential equality of blacks but still allowed segregation in schools and public places. It had meant that the blacks deserved equal facilities but that these facilities could still be separate from those of white people. Montgomery, like many cities in the South, was staunchly segregationist. Prejudice was a deeply and emotionally entrenched custom. Suddenly, as a result of the Court's decision, the prevailing attitude of paternal tolerance degenerated into irrational retaliations. Fear and suspicion, developed over many generations, exploded into a daily and permeating paranoia on the part of both races but mostly on the part of whites.

Through all this Martin was living his life, watching history, fulfilling his ministry at Dexter, developing his ideas. Finally and quite abruptly, Martin and his ideas were called into action. Martin responded.

The incident which gave being to Martin's choice and new understanding began as a result of one woman's refusal to move back from the front of a bus. It was an ordinary confrontation, well known to Martin. But Mrs. Rosa Parks was tired. She was tired of sewing all day, tired of being told when and where to sit, what and what not to say. She was weary of this struggle to comply. She simply gave up. She wouldn't budge. She would accept the consequences. It didn't matter any more.

Martin Luther King, Jr.

Rosa Parks was arrested and a bond of $100 was set for her release. E. D. Nixon, a civil rights activist, paid her bond and began calling for people to help challenge the case. Martin Luther King, Jr., received a call, as did Ralph Abernathy, a close friend and pastor of the First Baptist Church. A one-day bus boycott was staged to protest Rosa Parks' arrest as well as past injustices. The boycott was an overwhelming success. Out of the temporary **alliance** of Negro leaders developed a new organization called the MIA, the Montgomery Improvement Association. Electing Martin as their president, its members confronted the first question: whether the bus boycott should continue. Martin turned the question to his people.

Success had bound the spirit into a camaraderie, launching overwhelming support for continuing the boycott. Car pools were formed. Walking groups began. Hitchhiking became common. From as far away as Tokyo donations poured in. The buses remained empty. They would remain thus for 381 days. During this interval all Martin's understanding of satyagraha came into play. Martin was jailed and released for a minor traffic violation. His life was constantly threatened. His home was bombed, with Coretta and their baby barely escaping. Negro leaders and crowds of black people responded angrily, threatening to retaliate against whites. Martin preached the message that we must love where there is hate, that only love absorbs hate. Nonviolence prevailed. Later he would instruct his followers on their alignment with the **good cause** and the techniques consistent with it.

Meanwhile, Martin and 100 others were arrested and indicted for an old law which prohibited boycotts. Martin was convicted and charged $500. But this did not stop him. He appealed his case before a higher court. Now the entire nation was watching Montgomery. Buses were still empty. Business was failing. Whites were attacking with open and indiscriminate violence.

On December 21, 1956, the Supreme Court mandated desegregation of buses. Truth had won. Violence had not been the method. Martin and his people realized that had Martin considered his own personal life before the cause of right, no case or question would have ever been placed before our highest court. This small piece in the puzzle would not have been found. Still, Martin moved on from this success, preaching the nonviolent way, preparing his people for the reprisals sure to come. Though no drastic violence resulted that first day, Martin's anticipation was accurate. A wave of beatings, burnings of buses, shootings, explosions ensued. The world was watching Martin. How would this black Gandhi respond to this crisis?

As a response to this violence a new, more encompassing organization developed from a meeting of representatives from 10 states. The SCLC, the Southern Christian Leadership Conference, evolved, electing Martin Luther King, Jr., its president. Martin preached the doctrine and tactics of non-violence to this group, outlining the attitudes and techniques which interpreted Gandhi's satyagraha. They were to align themselves with what was right, following it wherever it led them, rather than reacting personally and emotionally to the violence. They would use boycotts, disobedience of unjust laws, sit-ins, protest marches, mass gatherings, pilgrimages. They would send petitions to their American leaders. They would withstand physical abuse, arrest, imprisonment, even death rather than meet the violence at its own level. Their cause would make its point known because it was right, not because it was capable of physically overpowering its opponents. An eye for an eye would only make the two sides become one mind eventually. Martin rejected this interpretation of justice.

Bombings of homes and taxis would consistently test this commitment. The Negro community waited, uncertain. Soon, however, the police intervened, arresting and indicting seven white men, convicting five and acquitting two. One battle against segregation and the mentality that had created it had been won. The violence subsided. Integrated buses—buses whose seating was open to all—began to roll. This crisis was over. The Negro community was acclaimed for its forebearance, for its mobilization and influence achieved through nonviolence though violence had been the white community's response.

King's next appeal was to the president of the United States. He felt that a strong statement of intent from Eisenhower would calm the mounting tension. Though a battle against segregation had been won, most of the schools in the South were still segregated. The 1956 Supreme Court decision on buses seemed a precedent for eliminating segregation completely. This was Martin's next concern. This was the white community's worst fear. But Eisenhower did not want to take such an obvious stand. He did, however, take an indirect stand on the issue of Negro voting rights by investing more authority in the Attorney General regarding the denial of voting. This would help later.

From these first few incidents and the rights which they eventually ensured, Martin Luther King, Jr., and satyagraha moved to requesting an unfettered ballot, school desegregation, and **integration**. The first march on Washington took place on May 17, 1957. Negro leaders and thousands of blacks and whites appealed to the government in a prayer pilgrimage before the Lincoln Memorial. In the years to follow, Martin also visited Africa, published his first book, and welcomed his first son. He was arrested for loitering at a courthouse while attempting to attend a trial, a mock charge designed to cause him hassle. Also, the first attempt on his life was made. A Negro woman who had claimed to be after Martin for six years stabbed him with an

Martin Luther King, Jr.

8-inch letter opener. The blade was so close to his aorta that had he even sneezed or coughed he would have died. Martin watched and waited calmly. It took four hours to withdraw the blade.

After a long convalescence Martin joined the cause again. He visited India, placing a wreath on Gandhi's shrine, discovering new understanding and resolve in the master's teachings. The people received the Kings with incredible openness. "In any other country," said Martin, "I come as a tourist; in India I come as a pilgrim." Later, after returning home, there were more arrests, court decisions, marches, lunch counter sit-ins, the student movement, freedom rides, threats and violent retaliation from whites. The violence was mounting in the late 1950s and early 1960s with more bombings, beatings, threats, and murders. Terrorism against the Negro community was the white community's answer to nonviolence.

Though disheartened many times, Martin continued his campaign for 10 years, transforming and elevating the Negro question to a national concern. Many small victories were won. Many people were enlightened. Many lives were lost despite the vow of nonviolence on the part of most of the Negro community. But always Martin pursued the true, the just, meeting the moment with his conscience, unafraid for his body, his employment, or his personal comfort. He felt that unless we were willing to stake our lives at some point, willing to die for something, we had not even begun to live. To shrink from our conscience for fear of physical, economic, or social reprisals was to Martin as it was to Socrates, to Thoreau, to Gandhi: more brutal a death than a physical death could ever accomplish. Martin knew death to be a constant, even an imminent possibility. He responded to this knowledge calmly saying he was not afraid to die.

That his cause was on the side of justice was further validated by both Presidents John Kennedy and Lyndon Johnson. Though many political and social forces tried to block the campaign, it was ultimately successful. Legal segregation was torn down. Voting rights were secured. Open violence against the Negro was punished. The Negro became at last what indeed he is, a person. Inherent in that personhood were all the rights and responsibilities of becoming an individual and a citizen. Though it would take many years to ensure this, Martin Luther King, Jr., opened the door.

It was August 28, 1963. Side by side stood black and white, men and women, children and grandparents. Servants and dignitaries, housewives and glamour girls, farmers and sports heroes, gas station attendants and actors were marching, appealing again to Washington in a voice 200,000 strong, saying before the pensive, saddened face of Lincoln, "We are here, and we . . . have a dream." Their spokesman, Martin Luther King, Jr., in an eloquent, impassioned speech, visualized the eternal dream. It was and is still a moving speech. It speaks to the heart, the oldest and most lasting intelligence. The heart knows the long road this dream has traversed.

" . . . We must forever conduct our struggle on the high plane of dignity and discipline. We must not allow our creative protest to degenerate into physical violence. Again and again, we must rise to the majestic heights of meeting physical force with soul force. The marvelous new militancy which has engulfed the Negro community must not lead us to distrust all white people, for many of our white brothers, as evidenced by their presence . . . have come to realize that their destiny is tied up with our destiny and their freedom is inextricably bound to our freedom. We cannot walk alone.

. . . I say to you today, my friends, that in spite of the difficulties and frustrations of the moment, I still have a dream. It is a dream deeply rooted in the American dream. I have a dream that one day this nation will rise up and live out the true meaning of its creed: "We hold these truths to be self-evident: that all men are created equal."

. . . And if America is to be a great nation, this must become true. So, let freedom ring from the prodigious hilltops of New Hampshire. Let freedom ring from the mighty mountains of New York. Let freedom ring from the heightening Alleghenies of Pennsylvania . . . .

. . . When we let freedom ring, when we let it ring from every village and every hamlet, from every state and every city, we will be able to speed up that day when all of God's children, black men and white men, Jews and Gentiles, Protestants and Catholics, will be able to join hands and sing in the words of the old Negro spiritual, " Free at last! Free at last! Thank God Almighty, we are free at last!"

A remarkable dream. A remarkable man. Perhaps the most remarkable quality in Martin's life, as in Gandhi's, was that he didn't set out in a fanatically or premeditated crusade, but developed his beliefs and tools slowly, thoughtfully, compassionately, yet fearlessly, always as a reasonable response to small, common incidents with principle rather than emotion guiding his actions. He was an ordinary man. It was the truth-force which elevated and magnified the cause and its consequences to a national barrier. Only truth drew its boundaries, destiny containing itself within and history transcribing.

It was 1968. This year Martin won the **Nobel Peace Prize,** the youngest person ever and the second black man to receive this award. Martin turned the tribute over to the 22 million black people who equally deserved the award. That same year he was struck down by an assassin's

Martin Luther King, Jr.

bullet at age 39. In a climate of shock and despair, an old green farm wagon pulled by two rangy brown mules—symbolic of the poor, the oppressed, the cause—threaded the streets of Washington bearing Martin's body home.

Free at last, Martin left to us an estate no will can justly appropriate. It is easy to assess and dispense with the car, the house, and the small bank account. However, assessing and dispensing with the spirit of such a man as Martin would prove an incredible and humbling task.

Vocabulary

reformer	sharecropper	passive resistance
integration	nonviolence	segregation
"good cause"	alliance	prejudice
NAACP	Nobel Peace Prize	commitment
crossroads	separate but equal	crusader

Martin Luther King Jr.: Transpersonal Domain:

contemplate at separate sittings.

while meditating:

experience your freedom to be yourself.

experience what you would feel like if you were never to be that self.

contemplate Martin Luther King's life.

contemplate Martin's dream.

contemplate a picture or drawing of his face.

During your daily meditation and your resulting insights about your own self, remember Martin's life and dream, how does your life realize or deny this dream?

Martin Luther King, Jr.

ACTIVITIES:
COGNITIVE DOMAIN
Knowledge—Comprehension—Application—Analysis—Synthesis—Evaluation

MARTIN LUTHER KING, JR.
Knowledge—Cognitive Domain
Recall how Martin Luther King, Jr., boycotted the buses.

MARTIN LUTHER KING, JR.
Comprehension—Cognitive Domain
Explain the background and the end result of the bus boycott.

MARTIN LUTHER KING, JR.
Application—Cognitive Domain
In what other instances have boycotts been effective? Ineffective? What conditions make a boycott effective? Why do these make it effective?

MARTIN LUTHER KING, JR.
Analysis—Cognitive Domain
Compare and contrast segregation in this country and South Africa's Apartheid. Give reasons for similarities and differences you discover.

MARTIN LUTHER KING, JR.
Synthesis —Cognitive Domain
Predict what would have happened and how history would have been different if Martin Luther King, Jr., had advocated violence. Develop a story, play, or videotaped presentation based on your prediction.

MARTIN LUTHER KING, JR.
Evaluation—Cognitive Domain
Evaluate the use of boycott as a political tool. Explain the strengths and weaknesses and advantages and disadvantages of a boycott.

MARTIN LUTHER KING, JR.
Knowledge—Cognitive Domain
Listen to, read, or recall Dr. King's "I Have a Dream" speech. Think of the meaning 'an eye for an eye.'

MARTIN LUTHER KING, JR.
Comprehension—Cognitive Domain
Restate what Martin Luther King, Jr., believed in.

MARTIN LUTHER KING, JR.
Application—Cognitive Domain
What personal, community or world conflicts might be resolved by the use of Martin Luther King, Jr.'s, methods? Explain how and why you believe this would work.

MARTIN LUTHER KING, JR.
Analysis—Cognitive Domain
Compare and contrast Martin Luther King, Jr.'s, methods and dreams with the concept 'an eye for an eye.' Explain similarities and differences between them.

Martin Luther King, Jr.

MARTIN LUTHER KING, JR.
Synthesis—Cognitive Domain
Formulate a plan for a nonviolent method to overcome some evil or wrong in the world, your school, your home. List the chain of events or effects that might accompany each step of your plan.

MARTIN LUTHER KING, JR.
Evaluation—Cognitive Domain
Evaluate the effectiveness of 'an eye for an eye' and King's dream for attaining one of your goals. Give the reasons why one method is superior to the other in this instance.

AFFECTIVE DOMAIN
Receiving—Responding—Valuing—Organizing—Characterizing

MARTIN LUTHER KING, JR.
Receiving—Affective Domain
Listen to or read the "I Have a Dream" speech.

MARTIN LUTHER KING, JR.
Responding—Affective Domain
Express to a friend the emotions this speech evokes in you.

MARTIN LUTHER KING, JR.
Valuing—Affective Domain
Decide how important the "I Have A Dream" speech has been to the Civil Rights movement. Explain how you decided on its value.

MARTIN LUTHER KING, JR.
Organizing—Affective Domain
Considering Martin Luther King, Jr.'s, life, the "I Have A Dream" speech and other speeches and actions, rank them in order of their importance. Explain your ranking.

MARTIN LUTHER KING, JR.
Characterizing—Affective Domain
Describe the world as it would be if everyone shared Martin Luther King, Jr.'s, dream. Give the reasons for the conditions you describe.

MARTIN LUTHER KING, JR.
Receiving—Affective Domain
Play the "Prejudice" game.
(In *Imagination and Language*, see General Resources.)

MARTIN LUTHER KING, JR.
Responding—Affective Domain
Write down all you felt and thought during the game.

MARTIN LUTHER KING, JR.
Valuing—Affective Domain
Based on your experiences when playing "Prejudice," decide how important equal rights are to you. Explain the reasons for your feelings.

Martin Luther King, Jr.

MARTIN LUTHER KING, JR
Organizing—Affective Domain
In what ways, if any, did playing "Prejudice" change your feelings about discrimination? Why? What might others learn from the game? Why would they learn those things?

MARTIN LUTHER KING, JR.
Characterizing—Affective Domain
Explain why "separate but equal" does not achieve true equality. Provide at least five reasons and/or supporting examples.

BIBLIOGRAPHY

Title: *Martin Luther King, Jr.: A Story for Children* (grades K-3)
Author: Margurite Thompson
Publisher: GAUS, 1983

Title: *Martin Luther King, Jr.—America's Greatest Nonviolent Leader in the Struggle for Human Rights* (grades 5-6)
Author: Valeri Schloredt
Publisher: Gareth Stevens, Inc., 1988

Title: *Martin Luther King, Jr.* (Biography) (grades 5 and up)
Author: Jean Darby
Publisher: Lerner Publications, 1989

Title: *Martin Luther King, Jr.—A Profile*
Author: Edited by C. Eric Lincoln
Publisher: Hill and Wang, 1970

Title: *Martin Luther King, Jr.*
Author: Margaret Jones
Publisher: Childrens, 1968

Title: *Martin Luther King, Jr.: A Biography for Young Children* (grades K-3)
Author: Schlank and Metzger
Publisher: RAEYC, 1988

Title: *Martin Luther King, Jr.— A Documentary—Montgomery to Memphis* (grades 8 and up)
Author: Edited by Flip Schulke
Publisher: Norton, 1976

Title: *Meet Martin Luther King, Jr.* (grades 3-6)
Author: James De Key
Publisher: Random House, 1969

Title: *Martin Luther King: The Peaceful Warrior* (grades 3-6)
Author: Ed Clayton
Publisher: Archway, 1989

Title: *The Man Who Climbed the Mountain: Martin Luther King* (grades 4-6)
Author: Gary Theis and Dan Paulsen
Publisher: Raintree Publishing, Ltd., 1976

Title: *Life and Words of Martin Luther King*
  (grades 7 and up)
Author: Ira Peck
Publisher: Scholastic Inc., 1986

Title: *Martin Luther King, Jr.*
  (Picture-Storybook biography)
Author: Margaret Jones
Publisher: Childrens, 1968

Title: *Martin Luther King, Jr., Young Man with a Dream* (grades 2-6)
Author: Dharathula Millender
Publisher: MacMillan, 1986

Title: *Martin Luther King, Jr.—Mini Play*
  (grades 5 and up)
Author: Black American Series
Publisher: Stevens and Shea, 1977

FILM
I Have a Dream

RESOURCES FOR TEACHERS

Title: *What Manner of Man: A Biography of Martin Luther King, Jr., 1929-1968*
Author: Lerone Bennett, Jr.
Publisher: Johnson Chi, 1968

Title: *Marching to Freedom: the Story of Martin Luther King Jr.* (grades K-6)
Author: Joyce Milton
Publisher: Dell Publishing, 1987

Title: *I Have a Dream*
Author: Lenwood Davis
Publisher: Greenwood, 1973

Title: *Martin Luther King Jr.*
  (Ebony Picture Biography Service)
Author: Ebony Editors
Publisher: Johnson Chi, 1968

Title: *Martin Luther King, Jr.*
Author: Nigel Hunter
Publisher: Bookwright Press, 1985

Title: *Martin Luther King, Jr.—An Annotated Bibliography*
Author: Compiled by Sherman Pyatt
Publisher: Greenwood, 1986

Title: *Martin Luther King, Jr.: A Profile*
Author: Eric C. Lincoln
Publisher: Hill & Wang, 1970

Title: *To Kill a Black Man*
Author: Louis Lomax
Publisher: Holloway, 1987

Martin Luther King, Jr.

Title: *Martin Luther King, Jr., The Making of a Mind*
Author: John Ansboro
Publisher: Orbis Books, 1984

Title: *Martin Luther King, Jr., A Man to Remember* (grades 4 and up)
Author: Patricia McKissak
Publisher: Childrens, 1984

Title: *Martin Luther King*
Author: Rae Bains
Publisher: Troll Associates, 1985

Title: *Search for the Beloved Community: The Thinking of Martin Luther King, Jr.*
Author: Kenneth L. Smith and Ira G. Zapp
Publisher: University Press of America

Title: *Political Philosophy of Martin Luther King, Jr.*
Author: Hanes Walton
Publisher: Negro University Press, 1971

Title: *Frame-Up: The Martin Luther King-James Earl Ray Case*
Author: Harold Weisberg
Publisher: Weisberg, 1971

GENERAL RESOURCES

BOOKS

Title: *As a Man Thinketh*
Author: James Allen
Publisher: Mind & Art Publishing, 1989

Title: *Towards a Psychology of Being*
(Excellent)
Author: Abraham Maslow
Publisher: Van Nostrand Reinhold Co., 1962

Title: *The Farther Reaches of Human Nature*
(Excellent)
Author: Abraham Maslow
Publisher: Penguin, 1976

Title: *Space-Time and Beyond*
(Interesting illustrations)
Author: Bob Toben
Publisher: E. P. Dutton and Co., Inc., 1975

Title: *Transpersonal Education: A Curriculum for Feeling and Being* (Excellent
essays and an extended bibliography)
Publisher: Prentice-Hall, Inc., 1976

Title: *Affective Education Guidebook*
(Great for activities, games, process, and introduction to meditation)
Author: Bob Eberle & Rosie Emery Hall
Publisher: D. O. K. Publishers, 1975

Title: *Imagination and Language*
(Excellent curriculum for Transpersonal Domain; includes "Prejudice Game")
Author: Linda Wermuth
Publisher: Prentice-Hall, 1976

Title: *The Hymn of the Universe*
Author: Pierre Teilhard De Chardin
Publisher: Harper & Row, 1969

Title: *Seeing with the Mind's Eye*
Author: Mike Samuels and
   Nancy Samuels
Publisher: Random House, 1975

Title: *How Your Mind Can Keep You Well*
Title: *How To Control Your Emotions*
Author: Roy Masters
Publisher: Foundation of Human
   Understanding, 1976

Title: *They Changed the World*
(Great short biographical sketches and paintings)
Author: Garfinkel
Publisher: Platt and Munk

General Resources

Title: *The Primal Alliance: Earth and Ocean*
Author: John Hay and Richard Kauffman
Publisher: Friends of the Earth

Title: *The Joys of Meditation*
Author: Justin Stone
Publisher: Sun Pub., 1975

Title: *Meditation for Little People*
(grades K-4)
Author: Anne Langford
Publisher: DeVorss, 1976

Title: *Handbook to Higher Consciousness*
Author: Ken Keyes, Jr.
Publisher: Love Line Books, 1975

Title: *Philosophy: An Introduction*
Author: John Herman Randal, Jr. and Justus Buchler
Publisher: Harper & Row, 1971

Title: *The Last Flower: A Parable in Pictures*
Author: James Thurber
Publisher: Harper Colophon Books, 1971

Title: *Tao Te Ching*
Author: Lao Tsu
Publisher: Random House, Inc., 1972

Title: *Modern Man in Search of a Soul*
Author: C. G. Jung
Publisher: Harcourt, Brace & Jonanovich, 1955

Title: *The Wisdom of Insecurity*
Author: Alan Watts
Publisher: Random House, 1968

Title: *Behold The Spirit*
Author: Alan Watts
Publisher: Random House, 1972

Title: *Meditation Cards*
(Excellent for teaching meditation)
Author: Anjanee Mata
Publisher: Laytonville, California, 1975

Title: *Grow or Die, The Unifying Principle of Transformation*
Author: George T. Ainsworth-Land
Publisher: Wiley, 1986

Title: *Trance, Art, and Creativity*
Author: John Curtis Gowan
Publisher: John Curtis Gowan Co., 1975

General Resources

RELATED LITERATURE

Title: *The Little Prince*
Author: Antoine de Saint Exupery

Title: *The Velveteen Rabbit*
Author: Marjorie Williams

Title: *Jonathan Livingston Seagull*
Author: Richard Bach

TRANSPARENCIES

Title: Art and Culture Series:
  Images of Nature, Images of Change,
  Images of Fantasy
Author: Sara Jenkins
Publisher: Milliken Pub. Co. Missouri, 1973

yourself

Love yourself and watch--
today, tomorrow, always.

First establish yourself in the way,
then teach,
and so defeat sorrow.

To straighten the crooked
you must first do a harder thing---
straighten yourself.

You are your only master.
Who else?
Subdue yourself
and discover your master.

        from: <u>sayings of the Buddha</u>

TAXONOMY OF COGNITIVE OBJECTIVES*

KNOWLEDGE .... LEARNING THE INFORMATION

COMPREHENSION .... UNDERSTANDING THE INFORMATION

APPLICATION .... USING THE INFORMATION

ANALYSIS .... EXAMINING SPECIFIC PARTS OF THE INFORMATION

SYNTHESIS .... DOING SOMETHING NEW AND DIFFERENT WITH THE INFORMATION

EVALUATION .... JUDGING THE INFORMATION

*Benjamin S. Bloom and Others, Taxonomy of Educational Objectives, Handbook 1: Cognitive Domain (New York: David McKay Company, 1956)

TAXONOMY OF AFFECTIVE OBJECTIVES*

RECEIVING .... STUDENTS ARE WILLING TO BE AWARE OF AN EVENT AND TO PAY ATTENTION TO IT.

RESPONDING .... STUDENTS REACT TO AN EVENT THROUGH SOME FORM OF PARTICIPATION.

VALUING .... THE EVENT HAS VALUE TO STUDENTS AND THEY TREAT IT AS A BELIEF OR WITH A POSITIVE ATTITUDE.

ORGANIZATION .... AS STUDENTS ENCOUNTER SITUATIONS FOR WHICH MORE THAN ONE VALUE IS RELEVANT, THEY ORGANIZE THE VALUES, DETERMINE THE INTER-RELATIONS, AND ACCEPT SOME AS DOMINANT.

CHARACTERIZATION .... STUDENTS CONSISTENTLY ACT IN ACCORDANCE WITH THE VALUES THEY ACCEPT AND THIS BEHAVIOR BECOMES A PART OF THEIR PERSONALITIES.

*David R. Krathwohl and Others, Taxonomy of Educational Objectives, Handbook II: Affective Domain (New York: David McKay Company, 1964)

MEDITATION AND THE TRANSPERSONAL DOMAIN

Though it seems a digression to introduce the Transpersonal Domain and meditation with a rationale, it is for some of us a reassuring toe in the water before we are ready to swim. The most noteworthy research and support come from many of our most respected and rigorous research scientists, but particularly Robert Ornstein. In his books *The Psychology of Consciousness* and *Mind Field* he provides sufficient reliable data asserting not only the two different modes of consciousness assigned to the two hemispheres of the brain, but also a delineation of the concerns and methods of each.

Oversimplified, the left hemisphere deals with a linear, rational (i.e., piecemeal) logic concerned with language, math, and intellectual thought. Its natural mode of expression is oral and written. The right hemisphere, on the other hand, operates from a nonlinear, intuitive. (i.e., holistic) and meaningmaking logic. Its expression or integration is inhibited by verbal and written translation, being expressed better in spatial movements, body coordination, empathy, living, and art. Further, Robert Ornstein maintains that Western culture has become hemiaopic, near-sighted, with one hemisphere overdominant. We emphasize the linear, rational, intellectual mode and devalue the nonlinear, intuitive mode. Many educators and social psychologists agree with this conclusion. They support his further assertions as well. Ornstein feels this hemiaopism has become so overbearing in some cases that we cannot even allow ourselves to consider cultivating our intuitive side because our linear-rational mode of thinking has blinded us into 'thinking' it out of existence. Since many truths and everyday understandings are perceived and integrated only through this mode of consciousness, as people we are only half developed when we disavow what is determined now as the balance of human awareness.

We know further that this mode, the intuitive, does and has always existed. It is the language of art, of the tonal qualities of music, of all forms of love, of religious insight, and the supposed 'esoteric' wisdoms of the East. Like any mode, art, or discipline it can and must be cultivated. Its method of cultivation is, however, radically different from the fostering of intellectual pursuit. First, trying to understand or experience the scope and validity of the intuitive with our intellect is like assuming we've been to Europe because we've read the travel guide. In one sense, an intellectual sense, we have. In the real, integrative sense, of course, we have not. Intuitive receptivity and understanding, like meditation and the Transpersonal Domain, is an

Meditation and the Transpersonal Domain

experience, a lifetime pursuit, and cannot be learned or taught except via our own personal relationship to them.

Many cultures of the East have valued this mode and we have much to gain by our association with their wisdoms. Ornstein rightfully warns us, however, against cultism, trying to exchange the intellectual mode for the intuitive, or donning garb, ritual, and lingo in order to appear as if we have made the transition. The goals of this Guide are consistent with this warning. If we can detach the content from the package of cultural wrapping or ritual, sensationalism, or the mask of personality, we can reap and facilitate the essence of available wisdom. The distillation can then be meditated on, tested in our own daily lives and cultures, and incorporated when known as valid. In this way we will culivate the balance between ourselves and our culture via the centuries of search which have produced this wisdom. Its timely nature is striking when we consider the abortive personal searches of our children which too often end in mindless cultism, self-indulgence and preoccupation, drugs, and at an increasing rate, suicide.

Cultivation and valuing of the intuitive mode through the Affective and Transpersonal Domains is a major concern of this Guide. All the people presented here attended to and achieved this balance and eventual transformation. We are concerned with their journey and their discoveries only insofar as they became part of our own 'conscious evolution' as an individual, a nation, or peoples of one planet.

> The right kind of educator, seeing the inward nature of freedom, helps each individual student to observe and understand his own self-projected values and impositions; he helps him to become aware of conditioning influences about him, and of his own desires, both of which limit his mind and breed fear; he helps him, as he grows . . . to observe and understand himself in relation to all things, . . . Freedom comes only when one understands the ways of the self, the experiencer. It is only through the experiencer that experience takes on an entirely different significance and becomes creation.
>
> J. Krishnamurti

What we seek, then, is transformation, a change in form, nature, or character. But how do we achieve it? This ability to transform our lives and the lives of others grows from many roots. Two of the roots we as educators have traditionally defined are the Cognitive and the Affective Domains, or functions. These correlate somewhat with the two hemispheres of the brain: the

Meditation and the Transpersonal Domain

left hemisphere—intellectual mode/cognitive domain—and the right hemisphere—intuitive mode/affective domain. As Ornstein reports, the cognitive or intellectual has been over emphasized. Many teachers now agree and are attempting to value feeling as well as thought. Still, to many of us, something is lacking.

It is the age-old argument: Is the whole equal to or greater than the sum of its parts? As was suggested earlier in the Genesis section of the Source Guide, we can view the Affective Domain as the 'person' and the Cognitive Domain as his or her 'tool.' With this view, anything manipulated in thought, the brain, must be interpreted by and integrated with the person, the heart. It was also suggested that to help fuse these domains, and to discover new ways to cultivate the Affective/intuitive, the Transpersonal Domain was generated. Yet to fully use this domain, this faculty, requires a unique curriculum, one whose method many of us have let decay, even for ourselves. It is a curriculum of the inner world, whose base is personal yet universal, whose stimulus and patterns of response are internal and, for most of us, still being discovered. This approach does not respond directly to the outside world but rather collates all facts, experiences and insights we have accumulated since birth, collaborating past, present, and future—eternity and the moment—personal and universal—positive and negative. It is not easily expressed in language, except perhaps in poetry and creative prose, but it is a knowing nonetheless valid. It uncovers meaning and purpose, resolves opposites, coordinates mind, body and spirit. It is that which we glimpse fleetingly, hearing ourselves or another calling it . . . essence.

In many cultures and religions, techniques for attending to this evolving essence have been provided. Some include chanting, visual or graphic enigmas, koans, music, riddles, concentration on one object or word, silence, fasting, and above all meditation. All are intended to get us out of our heads and into our hearts to experience what is central to the human condition. All these cultures knew that intellectual thought was not a proper approach and was often a hindrance. As stated earlier, though progress has been made in the area of intellectual accomplishment and interpersonal communication, modern man has disregarded the necessary freedom and cultivation of the intra-personal, as well as the transcendence of the merely personal. Supporters and risk-takers of transpersonal education believe a person can and must touch this base daily. Through the process of locating it and attending to it daily we begin our own transformation, overcoming fear and conditioning, discovering the flux of our own biases. Through the process we integrate intellectual and emotional response to the outside world,

Meditation and the Transpersonal Domain

becoming better able to unify with our own destiny and the fellows who share that life. All that remain are reality, choice, and each person's clear perception and intent.

The chief method by which this Source Guide hopes to accomplish these inner tasks is called meditation. It is a catalyst. Stated simply, meditation is learning to wait to receive. It is practicing: how not to get mired in one's thoughts, or on one thought; how not to identify oneself with one's thoughts, ultimately to direct one's mind; and, since one no longer dwells on one thought, or piece, or opinion, how to perceive and be creative in one's own being. This learning becomes a balance of the totality, or essence, of issues, of one's self, of the other, of truth, of reality. In this totality, choice becomes enlightened, as Krishnamurti said, "creation." Since choice is the vehicle by which we evolve as an individual, with conscience our guide, an enlightened conscience is an obvious asset.

In this Source Guide, meditation is a natural and necessary companion. The true aim of meditation is to lead the students back to themselves as they are. Then looking at others will naturally cause the students to examine themselves. If they find themselves by comparison falling short of something they can value but have no way to grow, we defeat our purpose. A self, preoccupied with self-recrimination, has taken one more step away from who it is right now, which is the only avenue to its actual and potential self.

With meditation, the student recognizes that all people who wish to become or transform themselves begin with themselves as they are. This means facing the same everyday, often petty, fears, desires, tempers, and details that the human being has always encountered. None of us escapes this. Meditation gives us a daily space to observe and take account of ourselves. The benefits of inner freedom give us a constant empty place to remember who we are: a place into which all experience can filter and be sifted; a place where pertinent insight might arise; a place from which all response can be initiated. Action becomes then a creative response, not a reaction.

But what is meditation? Philosophically it is a method meant to literally drive us out of our minds, that is, away from always or only operating from an intellectual mode. It aims at startling us from linear fragmented perceptions into holistic and sudden insights which erupt naturally as part of daily life. Physiologically, meditation aims at slowing down mental and metabolic functions, in changing the brain-wave pattern which expresses our conscious mode.

Meditation and the Transpersonal Domain

The mind and body will at first produce spontaneous thoughts and images and anxieties. As these come before the mind's eye, they are observed and released, not dismissed, just moved along so we can watch the entire cycle of thought itself. This practice "releasing" reacquaints us with the objective choosers—ourselves, and that which transcends even ourselves. Imagination will have its play but even fantasy must necessarily be relegated to a tool we can direct. Over the years, many levels are reached. Many stages of entrance are reached. Simply stated, one experiences first the calm, a euphoria, a mask of fear, a sense of the grandiose regarding one's own self, overwhelming sadness, and finally clarity. As time passes, the sensational results lessen into a natural way of cleaning house. We begin to see both the angel and the devil in us all. We move from self-recrimination to self-acceptance, from self-preoccupation to self-realization, and hopefully from illusion to reality and self-transcendence. The goal is not that the ego be annihilated but that we experience more than just our own ego.

Psychologically, meditation, as well as a time of reflections and contemplation, is a time of ceasing external stimuli. Meditation is the beginning time, a place, and an attitude we set aside each day. In this hollow space, insights, images, and ideas will present themselves, but there is no emphasis on response or expression. Response by its very nature short-circuits the complete cycle of thought and its transcendence. Expression holds onto a thought or image. The aim is to learn to release thought, to its process and our own conditioning. Eventually, this objectivity becomes a way of life with full expression in the details of living. But in the beginning, expression is reduced to a journal. This can be kept to record impressions, insights, and thoughts. A variation of meditation is programmed or contemplative meditation. It concerns guided meditations or meditations on sacred writings or pictures.

Currently, there are many forms of meditation being taught. Some are sensational, some are mysterious and secretive. One can begin very simply, however. One does not need to don costume or lingo. Just setting aside a time and place is a good start. Closing the eyes reduces visual stimuli, folding the hands helps give us a sense of containment. A clean, private place sets an environment of clarity. Soft, low music can make the initial silence more tolerable. Perhaps the most important element is consistency. Sometimes we feel like we get nothing out of our sitting, an obvious mental set of material exchange. But meditation has been compared by the wise to an empty field. The process of meditation is like plowing the field to prepare it for planting and the natural growth which follows. In a world so highly geared to a modern rhythm and rate of exchange, the contrast of silence and patience seems at first strange. It is not. We have only forgotten. Let us remember.

SUGGESTED AREAS TO BE PROCESSED THROUGH ALL THREE DOMAINS: COGNITIVE, AFFECTIVE, AND TRANSPERSONAL

INNER TASKS — TRANSPERSONAL

Try to spend at least 15–20 minutes daily within a receptive and relaxing environment.

Other kinds of meditation: receptive and programmed or contemplative.

Experience your breathing, pulse, body, sounds of the day, wind blowing.

Contemplate one quote or poem introducing each person, at separate sittings.

Contemplate each one's life or one experience in that life. Contemplate all of your past, or one memory; watch all your thoughts.

Contemplate your own face or body in the mirror.

Contemplate a portrait of each person in the book separately.

Contemplate NOW! This moment!

Contemplate a koan or haiku, a candle, an hourglass.

Experience a place, a piece of music or a feeling, and watch its process.

Remember a dream, re-enter it.

SUGGESTED AREAS TO BE PROCESSED THROUGH ALL THREE DOMAINS: COGNITIVE, AFFECTIVE, AND TRANSPERSONAL

	BUDDHA	GREEKS	THOREAU
	Life and Death . . . how did each view the following?		
COGNITIVE (Emphasize Expression)	4 noble truths Eightfold Path karma caste truth light and dark the way	Socratic method dialectic mission slaves world of forms highest good paradox existence epistemology empirical scientific method syllogism	self-sufficiency duty slaves individual ideals God reality existence nature civil disobedience friction
AFFECTIVE	truth mara meditation compassion middle way self follow heart follow the way	truth desires inquiry/self-examination truth moderation wonder oracle psyche, soul highest good real	potential mission/calling actualize reality, truth needs vs. wants inquiry/self-examination truth walking wonder conscience different drum

SUGGESTED AREAS TO BE PROCESSED THROUGH ALL THREE DOMAINS: COGNITIVE, AFFECTIVE AND TRANSPERSONAL

	GHANDI	RACHEL	MARTIN
	Life and Death... how did each view the following?		
COGNITIVE	satyagraha self-reliance dharma outcasts truth-force Rama right and wrong life boycott civil disobedience	duty/prophet dream outcasts life's perfection life DDT nature confront research ecology	dream segregation good cause God right and wrong freedom non-cooperation
AFFECTIVE	truth brahmacharya meditation ahimsa self and Rama duty/prophet dharma hold to truth	reality love wonder conscience purpose joy	truth love conscience be willing

Emphasize Expression

Also in the CREATIVE LIVES SERIES—

MUSICIANS: Exploring Music through the Study of Six Great Lives
by Chris Brewer (revised 1992)
This self-directed study unit introduces students to the elements of sound, instruments of the orchestra, elements of music, and six famous composers—Bach, Mozart, Beethoven, Debussy, Tchaikovsky, and Copland. Grades 2-6.
91 pages, 8 1/2" x 11", softbound.
ZS03-W . . . $14.95

ARTISTS: Exploring Art through the Study of Five Great Lives
by Chris Brewer (revised 1992)
Acquaint your students with the principles of design, the creative process, and five of the world's master artists—da Vinci, Homer, Picasso, Van Gogh, and Escher. Grades 2-6.
79 pages, 8 1/2" x 11", softbound.
ZS05-W . . . $14.95

REFLECTIONS ON WOMEN: Exploring Leadership through the Study of Five Great Lives
by Sally Patton (revised 1991)
Your students will not only research five exceptional women—Catherine the Great, Queen Victoria, Eleanor Roosevelt, Golda Meir, and Indira Gandhi—they'll also learn about monarchies and democracies from each woman's viewpoint. Grades 2-6.
68 pages, 8 1/2" x 11", softbound.
ZS08-W . . . $14.95

INVENTORS: Exploring Ingenuity through the Study of Five Great Lives
by Patton and Maletis (revised 1989)
Students examine the lives of Leonardo da Vinci, Benjamin Franklin, Alexander Bell, Thomas Edison, George Washington Carver, and the Wright brothers. Follow a time line of each inventor to find out how his creativity was affected by society and his environment. Grades 2-6.
72 pages, 8 1/2" x 11", softbound.
ZS01-W . . . $14.95

EXPLORERS: Discovering the World through the Study of Five Great Lives
by Chris Brewer (1993)
Inspire your students' explorations with these multidisciplinary activities. Your students can follow the paths of five great explorers—Christopher Columbus, Mary Kingsley who ventured into Africa, polar explorer Roald Amundsen, Jacques-Yves Cousteau, and astronaut/philosopher Edgar Mitchell. Grades 5-8.
104 pages, 8 1/2" x 11", softbound.
ZS09-W . . . $17.95

Presenting the GREAT IDEAS SERIES—

ARCHITEXTURE: A Shelter Word
by Patton and Maxon (revised 1989)
Students explore our need for shelter as well as the influence of the environment and culture on the architecture of the world. Subtopics include—Caves, Pyramids, Homes of Ancient Greece, Castles, and Traditional Homes of Japan. Grades 2-6.
54 pages, 8 1/2" x 11", softbound.
ZS04-W . . . $14.95

ALPHABETICS: The History of Written Language
by Sally Patton (revised 1989)
This historical perspective of our alphabet encompasses the study of its major contributors—Prehistoric People, the Sumerians, the Egyptians, the Chinese, the Greeks, and the Romans. Grades 2-8.
92 pages, 8 1/2" x 11", softbound.
ZS06-W . . . $14.95

To order, write or call—

ZEPHYR PRESS
P.O. Box 13448-W
Tucson, Arizona 85732-3448
(602) 322-5090 • FAX (602) 323-9402

You can also request a free copy of our current catalog showing other learning materials that foster whole-brain learning, creative thinking, and self-awareness.